First published by Zidane Press in 2010.

Zidane Press Ltd.
Unit 4. Olympia Trading Estate
London N22 6TZ.

Text© Richard Osborne
Text© John Reid
Text © Mary Reid
Illustrations© Isabel Wilkinson
Graphic Design by Hendrik Schneider
www.hohan.co.uk

Distributed by:
Turnaround Publisher Services Ltd.
Unit 3 Olympia Trading Estate
London N2Z 6TZ
T: +44 (0)20 8829 3019

British Library Catalogue in Publication data.
A catalogue record for this book is available from the British Library.

ISBN 9780956267801

STUFF
YOU NEED TO KNOW
FOR UNIVERSITY

by
Richard Osborne
John Reid
Mary Reid

www.zidanepress.com

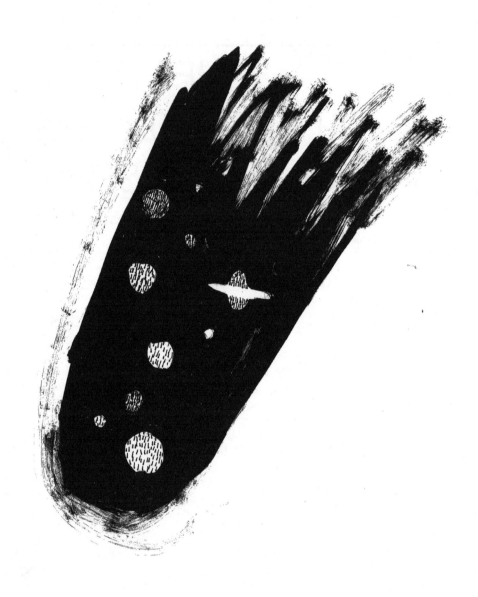

This book is the product of nearly 60 years combined teaching, studying and working in higher education. Its aim is to help you get through University in the most effective way possible.

The entire book condensed is: be there, do it, and finish - but you might want to look through some or all of the chapters, because you will find good advice and knowledge that will save a lot of time, energy and frustration whilst studying.

We aim to provide a mix of straightforward technical advice on how to study and also cultural information that will help the general process of acclimatising to university. There is clearly a lot packed into here, and some things will have been missed out, but in trying to cover huge areas you have to take risks. As teachers and ex-students we have tried to include everything we have discovered in those long years of reading, thinking and writing. In retrospect all three of us thought that if we had had a book like this right at the start we could have done better. Using the book is simple, you can just take the 'how to write essays' bit or read through the whole thing.

In three years at University if you don't find anything at all useful in this book then you are either Einstein or impervious to help.
Read, reflect and remember.

Content

The 10 Commandments

(or how to really do well at university)

I   Treat it like a job.

That is take it seriously and don't see it as an extended holiday with free loans. By this we mean nine to five, five days a week, to the best of your ability. If you develop a routine like this then all the aspects of the educational side of university become easier and more enjoyable. University is an opportunity which should not be squandered through getting wasted, and watching daytime TV with a hangover. The trick is to treat it like an extremely formative, rewarding and enjoyable job.

II   Go to everything.

Although this seems like a straight forward piece of advice we cannot reiterate enough 'GO TO EVERYTHING'. The majority of students have between fifteen to twenty hours of contact time a week, maximum. If you cannot manage to attend four hours of lectures and seminars a week then you are squandering the educational opportunity you have been handed. (You are also failing to comply with Rule No.1) Once you start missing things it becomes a habit. However hung over, if you are there some of the information will filter in.

III   Do not just use the internet.

The internet has existed for no more than twenty years and although it is the information super highway a lot of that information is not of the highest veracity or is, in other words, crap. The humble book, inhabiting the mysterious building labelled 'library' on your campus, is still a plentiful and vital learning resource which you need to use. Learning how to acquire knowledge first-hand is a key skill in University life.

IV Get involved with the faculty.

If the people teaching you know your name and can match it to your face, this is a positive. The same is true for you; get to know their names and faces. These people will be shaping your academic future so use them to the best of your advantage by making them do their job and teach you stuff. Attendance patterns correlate quite closely with eventual grades.

V Know your course.

Know when and where you have to be, what you are reading, who is teaching you and a basic outline of the upcoming topics. Not knowing these things was vaguely cute when you were entering secondary school but it is just pathetic when you are an eighteen plus first year university student. You are now on a competitive merry-go-round; those who know the most get the most.

VI Do all the reading.

This should be a given no matter what your course. A proportion of the undergraduate population will attend their lectures and seminars having read the blurb on the back of the book or nothing at all, do not let this be you. Doing the reading is essential and it should not be a chore seeing as you picked the course and the topic of study. The reading for your subject can be the most enlightening aspect of university but only if you enjoy it and thus give it the time and attention it deserves. Reading lists are often minimal; if you can't do that amount you perhaps should check out the rap-charts; that's the only place you get paid well for very short sentences.

VII Give yourself time.

The extracurricular parts of university; clubs, pubs, drugs etc are not things that this book suggests you steer clear of, but they are not the only facets of university life. If you wish to succeed academically and indulge in a fair amount of debauchery then working for set periods of everyday is far better than attempting to do everything in the twenty four hour period before it is due. You will learn more and your work will be of a higher calibre. Working hard and playing hard is a tricky combination; it can only be done by being either brilliant or very disciplined.

VIII Draft your work.

This should be second nature by the time you have got to university but, in case it is not, simply follow these instructions. Draft your work at least three to four times before you submit it. Make sure you know the referencing style that you need to use (consult the referencing section of this book to help you). The first thing you write down is not good enough, guaranteed, and spell check is not a drafting device.

IX   Meet Deadlines.

Deadlines at university are important. Not like A-levels when your nice teachers chased you up for work. No, you will fail the course, alienate yourself from your faculty and essentially screw yourself out of a decent degree. Get a diary and your course deadlines and know when your work needs to be in. If you can't meet deadlines eventually the line will go dead.

X   Do not lie to yourself.

There are many aspects to the overall university experience. If all are done in moderation and with a realistic view of their merits then it becomes exactly what it is sold as, a university EXPERIENCE. However, a great many students lie to themselves about a plethora of things such as use of time, work load, how much they smoke and drink and a host of others. This amounts to them not achieving what they are capable of. Be realistic and clear about what you want to gain from university and then put in the effort those goals require. Try the four day test - Have I been drinking and having a good time for four straight days? If the answer is yes then almost certainly you haven't been doing the coursework or the reading.

X (a) Enjoy Yourself.

This is vital, making friends and feeling comfortable in the university you have chosen are essential aspects to your over all enjoyment; but so is picking the right course. If you are doing Law and you want to be doing 18th century Russian History then you need to tell somebody and do something about it. Too many people hate their course and scrape through their degrees. You should not hate attending lectures, seminars and doing the work. If you do find something that enthrals then study that. If this decision upsets your parents then it is difficult but hopefully they will see that you fulfilling your potential is better than you resenting them for making you do a subject that you hate.

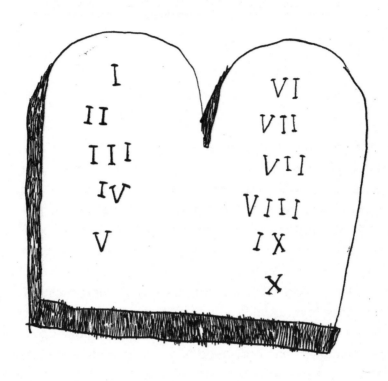

Studying expands knowledge, knowledge is power,
power corrupts, corruption is a crime,
crime doesn't pay. Why study?

Chapter 1.
The General Stuff

During the last two decades university education has changed dramatically, and is about to undergo another major change. From being an elite activity that involved a very small percentage of the population education has expanded dramatically and going to university has become the norm rather than the exception. In some ways it has become mass education and this has changed the nature of what goes on in universities. However the introduction of tuition fees has made it more difficult for working class students to achieve higher level qualifications and the threat of growing debt has dissuaded many from embarking on a three year 'booze up'. In general university enrolment has continued to increase as has the introduction of more subjects and broader areas of study, and this is clearly a good idea, but it does have its downsides. The recent introduction of 'top up fees' has further divided those whose parents could afford to pay up front and those with mounting debt and fewer job prospects. With this in mind Lord Peter Mandelson has recently spoken about a reformation of the university system. He proposes that students are consumers who should have access to all information about a university before they choose both their subject and institution. This information would include; dropout rates, contact hours with tutors, job prospects and estimated potential earnings. This (Mandelson presumes) would ensure young people make an educated decision on their futures prior to beginning their course. He also advocates a liberal first year in which students collect cultural capital from an eclectic choice of modules.

This would mean first years could study a combination of English, History, Economics, Philosophy, Science, Politics etc, before embarking on a more specific subject area in years two and three. Mandelson's arguments for the reformation of the university system are; to ensure that all people have an equal opportunity to attend further education and that they understand exactly what they will be getting. He also suggests that A Levels should no longer be the sole criterion on which young people are assessed. He wants institutions to take socio-economic factors into consideration when offering places. He requests that grade boundaries should be lowered for young people from failing secondary schools or difficult catchment areas. This would promote a diverse collection of students at the top universities such as Oxbridge, Edinburgh and Warwick.

Although this all sounds good, during an economic downturn when there are more unemployed graduates than ever before, any government in power is going to be looking to reduce the amount of tax payer's money that goes into universities. Mandelson's positive discrimination allowing more working class students into University is going to have to be paid for. The First Secretary of State proposes that tuition fees should be tiered dependant on your family income. This would make it more difficult for some students to gain grants and bursaries increasing the cost to study whilst ensuring a greater number of students from deprived backgrounds could achieve.

The new Coalition intends to massively reform higher education and fees will undoubtedly increase again. As a consequence of the new policy the redirection of young people away from academic study and into practical skills will take place regardless. In a post 'credit crunch' society routes of employment will change. Students will be expected to take part in work experience both at school and during their further study to ensure practical skills are learnt for the workplace.

Student Health

University is a breeding ground for germs. You collect hundreds of young people from around the country in one place, flood it with alcohol and hormones and *voilà*, the annual dose of Fresher's flu spreads through the university like wild fire. The general symptoms are those of the common cold but in addition to this you add exhaustion, a lack of fruit and vegetables and a persistent need to continue going out! It is usually around this time that your parents will receive a tearful phone call as the novelty of Fresher's week wares off and you are faced with taking care of yourself... well, in term time at least!

Mental Health

Your first year at university can come with high expectations of living alone, making large groups of friends and going out every night. However if this doesn't happen immediately your first few weeks can be lonely and spending time in your room may feel isolating. It is important that you do not let yourself become consumed with the feeling that you are the only student who hasn't made 'friends for life' on the first day. This is of course a myth and sitting alone in your new room is something that all first years have to realise is normal and essential to passing your degree. However, for some students these first few weeks are more than anxious as the change from their previous routine highlights a continuing low mood and depressive thoughts. For those who feel this, university offers a full range of different support options through both their medical centres and individual tutor support. Nationally there are also provisions in place for young people to find support whilst studying away from home. On the NUS website under mental health is a 'mood barometer' that displays the healthy fluctuation between feeling content to feeling low and how this changes regularly. It is when your mood is dominated by low and depressive thoughts that seeking assistance is a good idea.

http://www.nhs.uk
http://www.youngminds.org.uk
http://www.nus.org.uk/Campaigns/Student-Mental-Health/
The-mental-health-barometer

For the majority of students keeping optimistic and active is enough to sustain a positive state of mental health. Here are some tips on how to keep a health body and healthy mind.

Eat well: Fruit and Veg. It doesn't count if it's potted and microwaved! 5 Fruit and Vegetables a day.
Keep active. The student lifestyle is famous for turning skinny freshers into chubby second years in the blink of an eye. Exercise is healthy for body and mind and with cheap university gym membership you have no excuse!
Tidy up, wash your bed sheets, vacuum and you will feel happier and more organised.
Take a break from learning or drinking. Going for a walk, going to the cinema or spending time with friends will give your system time to recover.
Socialise. University is the perfect chance to meet new people with similar interests. If you're having trouble making friends join a society. Either get involved in your subject area or pursue another interest. Talking is very therapeutic and can encourage positive mental health.
Spend some time thinking about the good things in your life. You have made it to university which is a success; use that to motivate all areas of your life.
Get plenty of sleep. Eight hours a night will help you to think clearly and focus on working and playing hard.

General Health

The best way to maximise the amount of fun you have at university is to stay healthy. Take care of yourself and try and have a daily routine that includes sleeping and eating well. If you do get ill then stay in and recuperate. If you pick up something contagious then a weekend at home doesn't hurt and stops it spreading throughout your halls. Let's hope you never have to read this part of the book...

Sexual Health

Gathering thousands of young adults in one place and adding a variety of stimulants is a recipe for promiscuity. However, this should not mean that you are faced with a) STI's and b) Babies! In other words practicing safe sex benefits all involved. With diagnoses of Chlamydia in 15 – 25 year olds continuing to rise, universities are promoting sexual health clinics and free testing. Use them and arm yourself with all possible birth control and sexual health options.
There are many birth control options a few of which are listed below. However, a condom is the safest way for heterosexuals and homo-sexuals to prevent transmitting and contracting STIs.

Popular forms of contraception are:

Male and female condoms – create a barrier against sperm and the contraction of STIs.

Combined contraceptive pill – pill taken every day for 3 weeks, protects woman against pregnancy.

Contraceptive implants/ injections – injection works for 12 weeks and protect the woman from pregnancy. Implant works for up to 3 years but can be removed. Neither protect against STIs.

Contraceptive patch – worn on a patch of clean dry skin and replaced once a week; protects woman against pregnancy. Does not give protection against STIs

Diaphrams and Caps – prevents sperm from passing into the womb. Only gives limited protection against STIs.

You can get guidance online at www.nhs.uk and ask you GP about your nearest sexual health clinic.

Important Websites

The Gale literature resource centre: Directly accessible texts and MLA bibliography.
www.gale.cengage.com

Online worldwide catalogue (British Library catalogue):
www.ubka.uni-karlsruhe.de

Access to global newspaper articles and reviews
www.lexisnexis.com

Film database with access to the British film institute:
www.bfi.org.uk

Early English books online:
eebo.chadwyck.com

Referencing and style guide:
owl.english.purdue.edu/owl/resource

Chicago institute referencing and style guide:
chicagomanualofstyle.org

Unicef world statistics:
www.unicef.org/statistics/index.html

Food and Agriculture organisation of the United Nations:
www.faostat.fao.org

World statistics and country comparisons:
www.nationmaster.com

Organisation for Economic *Co-Operation and Development:*
www.oecd.org/home

National Union of Students:
www.nus.org

Students against depression:
www.studentdepression.org

Skills for Study:
www.skills4study.com

Universities UK:
www.universitiesuk.ac.uk

Chapter 2.
Fresher's week

Having very carefully chosen your institution, course and modules, finally arriving at University can be daunting. You have just read 100 books over the summer and memorized half of them, so you are nearly ready. Having battled all of the forms, loan arrangements, selling your soul to the government and other trivia involved with moving to a completely new place, you actually arrive. Basically for most people this means moving out of home for the first time.

The part where your parents drive you there and drop you off can be tricky as it is quite important to pretend that, in fact, they aren't your parents but either the hired help or some vaguely distant relatives who just happened to be there. (Some people manage it on their own!). The anxiety of all of these things is partly mediated by the excitement of it all, but it is pressure.

Again anticipating this and thinking about how you will deal with it is a very good idea. It is a fact that many first year students have not really thought about the complicated changes they are about to enter into. Having an idea of what might happen next is actually a very key skill for life in general – so it might be an idea to spend some time working out what you will do when you get to university. The pressure and stress is made worse by the demands felt in Fresher's week to have the maximum amount of fun and drink the most amount of alcohol possible (somewhere it was written that this is the truth of the quaintly named Fresher's week). Actually for most students it is an anxiety provoking time of trying to make friends whilst nursing an unpleasant hangover. This is to be expected, no one, however hard they try to prove otherwise is completely at ease with the situation.

Unhelpfully groups of second and third years run Fresher's events filled with stories of their 'incredible' first year fun week which was 'awesome' and 'carnage'. This just masks the true sense of relief they feel having now established a friendship group. The truth about your first week at university is that it is an experience that will come to an end and when it does you will feel a sense of accomplishment which will lead you nicely into the welcome structure of lectures and seminars. If you are armed with this information then it will be a breeze. Just be calm and talk to everyone you can, you're all in the same boat. It is also possible, given that everyone can be different, to not even go to Fresher's week because you were too busy doing the course reading.

You will make friends...

Another important thing to remember about your first weeks is that the people you are thrust into living with or those you meet whilst registering for your NUS card are not necessarily 'friends for life'. These 'friends' may turn out to be the people you hide from behind books in the library or nod to when walking around campus. The lifelong friends that you will no doubt make at university will find you slowly throughout your three years, on courses and in lectures, at the student's union or in the societies you join. It is very important that you don't commit yourself to superficial friendships made to get you through your preliminary weeks, and that you are patient. Deciding to live with someone in year 2 before Christmas is generally a disaster. When you return from the Christmas break you are no longer caught up in the first term bubble that clouds your judgement and you're more likely to make good decision about the people you want to live with. Don't forget familiarity breeds indifference. Fresher's week is also a good opportunity to join things and do things that you might not have thought you wanted to do, try being outlandish and joining the ballroom dancing society, or the sheep-shearing society, you never know.

Making a good impression:

When arriving at university there are a few necessities that will ease you into student life and break the ice between you and your new flat/house mates. Just remember to take your time and that getting so drunk that you can't find your way home is not the only sign of a good week. Also remember that sharing a flat with other people can be almost as difficult as taking part in Big Brother.

The general point that is being made here is that the whole new experience can be quite bizarre but if treated in the right way is great fun. This is the beginning of a major transition in life so it should be difficult. It is an experiment however and simply the beginning of a more complicated process. Think of it as a kind of speed dating with the entire population. Once you get over it you can start being a proper student, which is what the next chapters deal with.

For your own benefit take:

A duvet cover and pillow.

Some posters (otherwise your room will look like a prison cell).

Pictures of home (to help if you feel homesick).

Washing basket (essential if you don't want your whole room to become one).

Tea (many friends are made over a cup).

A critical sense of humour.

Here are some other well thought out tips:

Do not mention your Mum every 5 minutes
as this does not impress anyone.

Hide the fact that you brought your teddy bear/
Transformer with you, or that you have
Winnie the Pooh underpants.

It is permissible to exaggerate a little about
who/what you are. "My Dad is Simon Cowell",
even if true, should not be used as
an opening gambit.

Take any freebie anybody offers you.

Avoid credit cards; they are poison.

Say little and you will appear wise.

Carry a copy of Camus with you
everywhere you go. He is cool.

Be very careful of your possessions,
theft is endemic (have insurance).

Go to everything, talk to everyone.

Try not to remember anything about
the entire week.

Take with you:

A couple of bottles of wine
(or your drink of choice)

A bottle opener (because your flat
cannot be the only one without)

Can opener (because the contents of tins will
make up much of your first term diet)

Paracetamol (to ease the pain of your
hangover or those around you)

Your own mug (you will need
something from home)

More than one of everything so you can
invite people to dinner

Alarm clock, so you know what time it is
A calendar: so you know what date it is

Some kind of fancy dress costume
(because dressing as a school boy/
girl is a fresher necessity)

Chapter 3.
The Real Stuff

You are now on a course and have been given masses of information about the modules, reading, lectures, etc (or you should have been). This is the crunch point when the very well assisted sixth form stuff falls away and you are actually on your own. For various reasons many first year students don't get to grips with what is going on for quite a while, if ever. This should be avoided at all costs.

Once you are actually on the course, reading the books and going to all of the seminars and lectures you will need to produce fairly professional pieces of work. If, by some mysterious mishap, you didn't acquire this skill at 'A' level then here is a straightforward and sensible guide to how to do it. It is a sad fact of life that many students don't seem to work out what to do until their second or third year. Use this chapter to avoid acute inconsistencies. Remember, if you treat this like a job, you should be aiming to produce competent work on a regular basis.

(It is worth pointing out that some employers actually think a lot of graduates aren't quite top executive material). This section of the book may not be the most entertaining but it is probably the best value.

Referencing styles, Learning and Choosing subjects:

1. To achieve at University it is vital to choose the right course. If you spend three years dreading every lecture then your chances for success are limited. To make sure you have chosen correctly go to the first three weeks of lectures. If you understand nothing or hate everything you hear, then you are on the wrong course and this is the time to change.

2. It is a common mistake to choose modules purely on their title. 'Image, Vision and Dream' may sound inspiring but it is vague. The title doesn't always reflect the course content. Read the description and reading list, assess whether you would be able to fulfil the course criteria.

3. When choosing your modules, look at the breakdown of marks. Do not choose a module assessed 80% by exam if you don't perform well in a pressurised situation.

4. University is a big step up from A levels, albeit one you are no doubt ready to make. Prepare yourself for this by increasing your reading and looking at critical theory as well as novels. It is helpful to understand reading around the subject before having to start your first essay.

5. Go to seminars, lectures, meetings and tours in your first week. Fresher's week is not purely a test for your liver and can also be used to find your way around the campus and to your lecture theatres.

6. A common misconception passed down to first year students from wise (22 year old) graduates is that you only need to achieve an average of 40% to pass your first year and continue with your course. Although this may be technically true, your first year is an opportunity to read and explore your subject whilst ensuring your department know at least that you take their subject.

7. Whilst in seminars and lectures listen and take notes. Your lecturer has a greater knowledge base than you do. You can use their ideas as a guide to writing your essays, this is not plagiarism it's common sense. This does not mean writing down everything they say but creating phrases to trigger your memory.

8. Invest in a least one large ring binder, dividers and pens. It is not a good start to have to ask for a biro!

9. Finally, choose your essay questions early. If you do not understand the question allow yourself time to ask your seminar leader.
(They are reluctant to help if asked 24 hours before the deadline!)

University grading:

1st Class honours: 70% +

Given for going above and beyond. A complete answer to the question that creates a balanced argument. To accompany this; a full and detailed bibliography, grammatically flawless text and consistent referencing. A 2:1 with all the trimmings.

2:1: 60%-69%

Can be considered the equivalent of a B grade at A level. This is awarded for a solid essay with a developed argument. Although it has answered the question it has failed to convince the marker it deserves the highest award. An incomplete bibliography, lack of attention to grammatical detail or inconsistent referencing may be a reason for deducted marks.

2:2: 50%-59%

Awarded for an essay that has addressed the main themes of the title without creating an established argument or making a clear point.
The writing style may outshine the content or vice versa.
A 2:2 shows inconsistency in style and content.
OR
A strong argument and established writing style all put together in under 24 hours... Your lecturers know!

3rd: 40%-49%

Given for essays that do not meet the brief. An incomplete argument combined with a lack of research and content. Poor referencing and an inadequate bibliography may hinder the essay.
Getting one 3rd is not the end of the world, it points to a lack of direction in the essay and a misunderstanding of the key points of the module. Talk to your seminar leaders and sort the problem quickly. Then forget you ever wrote that essay!

Fail: 40% and below

Rarely given in the first year but if awarded the essay has failed to reach the required criteria of the course. A lack of bibliography or dubious referencing could make passing the essay impossible.

This may seem boring but if you actually know how essays are marked you will be able to get better grades, which presumably most people want. It is important to remember that you have achieved the grades to enter university and therefore you are intelligent enough to complete the work and pass. It is now up to you; writing essays with a hangover is not conducive to 1st class honours.

(Some universities move everything up by 15% as in the American system- known as grade inflation)

Some more rules:

1. Students should always keep asking questions until they are clear about what they should be doing.

2. Never believe rumours spread by other students about either essay writing or about copying.

3. Remember that plagiarism software is now very fast and accurate.

4. When writing essays don't try to be too clever, total originality will freak out your tutor.

5. Remember that you are a consumer as well as a student and you have rights. If something is not done properly on your course you can appeal.

6. Always communicate with your tutors about anything that is a problem, leaving it could make it worse.

Writing the Essays

Style and Formatting your Paper

When writing an academic paper it is crucial that the marker is presented with a clearly formatted piece of text. The way that this text is presented is dependent on your department's guidelines. Here are some suggestions as to how best to set out your work but it is important to remember that the university's way is the right way so yet again, learn it and stick to it.

Before writing your first essay the faculty should specify whether they require you to produce a front cover including: your name, your seminar leader's name, your course code and the title of your essay/ paper. Alternatively your department will provide you with a cover sheet so you can fill in the relevant information.
It is also advised that you insert a header onto every page including your name, course code, seminar leaders name and the course title so that this information appears on every page. This will help your work find its way to the right marker.

Consistency is the key to formatting your essay. Similarly to referencing if your marker can see you have made an effort to ensure each page is uniform then the placement of the required elements is superficial. Creating a piece of work that is clear and organised will be appealing to the markers eye and avoid confusion over cited and original passages of text. Here are a few tips to ensure your work at least looks the part.

Double Spacing. This allows the marker to write around the printed text, making notes for your benefit and to remind themselves of good and bad points. Your essay may not be accepted if not adequately spaced.

When choosing a font make sure that it is clear, each letter is separated and it is no smaller than 12pts. Times New Roman is universally used as it is clear to read.

Page numbers are a crucial tool for markers who may take the staples out of your work before reading it. When handing in your essay it is important to make it as easy for your marker as possible. Page numbers order your work so place them in one corner of each page. (This will also help you when re-drafting).

Justify your work. This makes the paper look complete, is visually pleasing and gives a clear margin for marking.

Indent the first line of a new paragraph by one inch. This is five spaces on the spacebar or one Tab.

Italics should be used to distinguish between normal prose and the title of a longer piece of work, media, fiction etc. This is approved by MLA to provide enough difference from plain text to make it stand out. Italics should be used as opposed to underlining which can make your paper look untidy.

Although the use of capital letters should be elementary, misplacing capitals is a persistent undergraduate fault. Your seminar leader will mark you down for grammatical errors including the misuse of capitals. They should only be used when signifying the name of a place or person. They may also be used when quoting from the title of another source. They should not be used to signify an important word or section.

Bibliography /works cited list

Your faculty will provide you with guidelines to formatting your essay and referencing your cited work. These will include instructions on whether to include a works cited list in addition to a bibliography.

Bibliography

The job of a bibliography is to indicate to the reader the depth and diversity of research done in order to write the essay. This will allow the marker to assess your understanding of the title dependant on the research used and cited. It can also act as an essential tool of referencing as it contains the information needed for the marker to locate the original works. The name, stated at the beginning of each source and arranged in alphabetical order in the bibliography acts as a key to the 'Harvard Style' or 'Author-Page' style of citations. This allows the marker to read the quote within your essay, note the author's name the beginning of the title and locate this in the bibliography.
The bibliography is not simply a list of the works included in your essay but may contain all work read in preparation for the essay. This could include multiple editions of a particular text, text books, film clips, websites, articles etc. Although all of these works may not be cited within your essay it is important for the marker to be able to map your research in order to assess your work.

Arrange the information in your bibliography in alphabetical order:

Author surname. Initial. (Year of publication) *Title of Work*. Place of Publication: Publisher

Example A:
Osborne, R. (2008) *Philosophy in Art*. London: Zidane Press

Example B:
Osborne, R. Van Loon, B (2004) *Introducing Sociology*. London: Icon Books

Works Cited List

As well as the inclusion of a bibliography some faculties ask for a list of cited works. This is formatted in numerical order in conjunction with the references throughout your text. This gives the marker a concise list that enables them to find the original version of the borrowed work. It is imperative to include a bibliography if a work cited page is required as this will give your marker a broader view of the research undertaken.

Quotes

Long Quotes: Prose
Long quotes consist of works from another source added to your text that are four lines or over of prose as seen in the original copy. When adding these quotes to your text they must be separated from the main body and indented. It is not necessary to use speech marks to highlight the quote.

Example:
Levi confronts the changing society.

> In June 1942 I spoke frankly to the lieutenant and the director: I realised that my work was becoming useless, and they too realised this and advised me to look for another job, in one of the not too many niches the law still granted me. (Levi, 91)

His admittance of the changing laws causes a profound change in his life.

Long Quotes: Verse
If the original text is in verse then the same rules apply. End each line of the text as the original does so.

Example:
Ceila disapproves of Roselind's use of disguise to trick Orlando.

> You have simply misused our sex in your
> love-prate: we must have your doublet and hose
> plucked over your head, and show the world
> what the bird hath done to her own nest.
> (Shakespeare Anthology, 236)

Short Quotes: Prose

Short quotes are under four lines long in their original format and may be inserted into your body of text. Unlike the long quotes, speech marks are required.

Example:
Orwell's understanding of the political climate is clear: "One is practically obliged to take sides, and it must be clear enough what side I am on." (Orwell, 231) There is no doubting his political alignment.

Short Quotes: Verse

Follow the same rules for adding text in verse with the addition of / to indicate the ending of each line.

Example:
Hamlet's speech begins: "To be or not to be that is the question/ whether 'tis nobler in the mind to suffer/ The slings and arrows of outrageous fortune" (Shakespeare Anthology, 886) displaying his attempted examination of human existence.

Follow the rules, know what is expected of you and you will achieve regular high grades – it is as simple as that.

Time managment is critical

Try and Get up before 12 am on a normal weekday.

Don't Stay up all night watching crap TV.

Work backwards from the end date.

Always have a Plan B. Prioritize essays are above parties.

Time Management.
One of the key skills in adult life, particularly in the real world work situation

Buy a wall chart.
Put deadlines, seminars and lectures on it.

Be Realistic.
Try planning one day in terms of how long things take (many people have never done this).
Then think about how long preparing a first essay draft takes, including research.
Consider how many essays you will have to do over a year.
If you use a wall planner and out deadlines in red you will start to get a picture.
Think about work avoidance things that everyone does to waste time (smoking).
Maybe schedule in 5 hours of real work each term day.
Do It Now.

Late Essay excuses:
                    Cry!!!

            My Dog Ate My Laptop
            (following up the next week
            with My Dog Died)

               Woman Trouble
            (can be used by both sexes
            just change the emphasis)

              Hand in blank page
    (claim that it is a post modern expression
      and that if you don't at least pass
          then your teacher is a Nazi)

              He stole my essay
     (point at weakest/ brightest student)

              Orangutang flu
    (rare, dangerous, contagious by paper)

              I can't write...

          Say: You know weed right..?
    (if they answer yes; look mournful and shrug)

Chapter 4.
Humanities;
An Overview

In the past when you went to university you used to be pushed into
selecting a course, a discipline or a joint degree, as they used to be
called. Now, however, there are increasingly wide choices and more
general options open, so investigate them. Modern universities have
changed a great deal in the last twenty years, from being elevated
centres of higher learning, what were called the 'Ivory towers', in which
the supposed academic elite studied the best of all things, to being
much more broadly educational. Back in the 1960s about 3% of
people went to university and they had sherry parties and were quite
intellectual in an old fashioned way. (Read the novel *Lucky Jim* by
Kingsley Amis to get a picture of this era). Now the point of university
is to give a good education to a massive 45% of the young population
(and getting towards 50%). Since 1997 when the blessed Tony Blair
got into power education has become a really big thing; some say it
has become a big business. Universities have grown hugely and so
classes and lectures have got bigger as well, which may or may not be
a good thing. It's worth knowing before you go to university that this
isn't Oxford that you're going to with punting and crumpets for tea and
stuff, as glamorised in *Brideshead Revisited* but a large corporation
whose business is education and may well be more like IKEA than some
charming little college with flowers in the entrance. Having realistic
expectations of what it is going to be like is probably a bit depressing
but may help the shock when you arrive with the other 22,000

students at a giant new building. What you need to know when you go to university is that to get the most out of it you are going to have to be clear about your aims, and quite pushy about getting what you are entitled too. As we said earlier be very sure that the course you are on is the right one.

In this chapter we are going to run through a general idea of what the humanities are about, how it developed and what sort of ideas are useful (and necessary) to be familiar with. By the end of the chapter you should have a vague sense of some key ideas, and trends, in the humanities and be able to recognise the essential key thinkers. In Western society it used to be known as the Greeks to the Geeks, a short history of Western civilization, but that has got a little more complicated now. The humanities in general could be described as the study of the many ways in which people process, react to and document the human experience. In other words what humans do and how they live and think. Since humans invented language and culture, we have used myth, literature, philosophy, religion, art, music, history and poetry to understand and record our experience. All of this falls into the general definition of the humanities. To have a map of how to navigate the terrain of the humanities is a useful back-up in a complex world.

The over-arching question in the humanities is that of how humans think, explain and picture their world, in different times and different places. It can also be the question of "Where do ideas come from?" It pretty much goes back to Socrates who asked the question, "What is Man?' followed by the very important question "What does it mean to act ethically". Being self-reflective about being human is the core of the humanities. The development of the different disciplines of the humanities is in itself an area of study, of plotting intellectual history. Having a sense of the development of human culture is fairly necessary background to the humanities.

Put more precisely the humanities set out to examine how we construct our aesthetic, intellectual, psychological, ethical, social, and political worlds, and to do so comparatively. At university you will be expected to go beyond looking at small areas of a particular discipline and to develop an overview of the differences between approaches in different times and places, and for different people.

Discovering how it all works is part of the fun of good teaching and learning. In general the humanities rely on methods of inquiry that are specific to this area. They are:

Analytic *understanding how literary and linguistic effects function.*

Inductive *drawing rational conclusions from evidence.*

Critical *making judgements about the value of things.*

Evaluative *comparing one sort of thing to another.*

Interpretive *analysing what things mean, and showing why.*

These approaches are markedly distinct from the empirical methods of the natural and social sciences, but this separation may be in itself an historical problem.

Sometime around Erasmus and the Renaissance, this separation began to develop between subjects which had previously all been inter-related where "hard" was divorced from the "soft" sciences and the arts. This division grew post Enlightenment and is still visible both geographically and intellectually on university campuses, as well as within the disciplines themselves.

The contemporary question in the humanities is whether the digital age is re-writing all of the scripts so that the arts and the sciences are re-combining.
There is an argument that the limitless possibilities of emergent technologies and humanities scholarship will produce a new field of inquiry that is the new humanities. Whichever way you approach it the humanities is a very different place to what it was just twenty years ago. It has been called the 'Big Humanities' by some contemporary theorists. Overall the humanities is about thinking in the most general sense about the human experience, what it has been and what it could become. That is why it is always relevant.

A condensed version of the Intellectual History of the Western World (excluding Babylon)

Homer did a lonely planet Odyssey
Which covered all humanity.
Christianity started out all radical and hope
And ended up as just a reactionary Pope.
Luther rejected all this indulgent crap
And started a thing called the Reformation Rap.
Swiftly followed by the Renaissance revival
Which emerged from ancient Greek's survival.
Protestantism popped up as a new ethic
And proved that clerical control was pathetic.
Individualism was all the rage
And Capitalism its newest phase.
Marx and Weber had opposing views
On how modernity got in the news.
Freud said it was all about dreams
And Einstein said time ran in streams
Technology transformed all communication
And postmodernism produced disinformation.
The digital age rewrote the rules
And disciplines became outmoded tools.
But hey ho do not such changes leave you out of sorts
Cos Shakespeare said it all in his weekly reports.
(And a woman said 'What about us?')
And then everyone began to cuss.
This is post everything, and the last post rarely come
Which is why, on the sly, humanities is us.

Chapter 5.
Literature, Books
and Plays

You may have signed up at university to study 'Literature' or English, as it was sometimes called, or Literary Studies or even Post-Colonial Literature; this chapter will look at the key points of that activity. Novels have always been profoundly important ways of thinking about the world and story- telling in the widest sense is a fundamental human activity. The story of the development of the idea of literature as a discipline has always been fixed on grand ideas, Mathew Arnold famously argued that studying literature was better than religion.

Later the grand old moralist F.R. Leavis, from the 1930s, continued this argument. He claimed that utilitarian values had so throttled the life force of twentieth-century culture, that it was only in reading really great literature that our moral and spiritual bearings could be recovered. Recently, the more politicised side of 'literary theory' (though in itself a beast with many shapes) proposed cultural criticism as a way of resisting ideological incorporation into the dominant ideologies.

The real point of reading literature is to discover "other" viewpoints and to see it as a means of thinking about how others percieve the world. This can be more complicated than it sounds. Recently some critics have argued that all fiction has been superceded by the strangeness of contemporary culture, which is awash with celebrity, weirdness and hyper reality 'the death knell of the novel.

.Literary Movements

Romanticism: 18th to 19th Century – Emphasising emotion and imagination rather than logic and scientific thought.

Pre-Raphaelite: 19th Century – Primarily English, undoing innovations by the painter Raphael – Painters and Poets.

Transcendentalism: 19th Century – American movement - Concerned with self-reliance, independence from modern technology.

Realism: Late 19th Century – based on simplification of style and image and an interest in poverty and everyday concerns.

Naturalism: Late 19th Century – Seeks to replicate a believable everyday reality. Heredity and social environment determine ones character.

Symbolism: End of 19th Century – French Movement Based on structure of thought rather than poetic form or image.

Modernism: Late 19th Century, Early 20th Century – Encompassing primitivism, formal innovation, reaction to science and technology.

Dada: Anti-art, focused on going against artistic norms and conventions. Started during WW1 peaked just after.

Surrealism: French movement, influenced by painting, uses surprising images and transitions to play off formal expectations and depict the unconscious mind.

Postmodernism: Post war movement, sceptical of absolutes and embracing diversity, irony and word play.

Homer

Argument rages about the actualities of Homer's life, about the nature of his existence and about his authorship of these epic works. What is evident is that his work occupied a central position in ancient Greece, shaping the development of Greek culture. The fact that these works have lasted to the present day is an indication of their brilliance and their importance. There is little bias and didactic effect in the works as they present human emotion and feeling. The lasting effect can be seen in the work of those that they have influenced such as Milton, Dante, Joyce, Woolf, Eliot, Freud and many other figures central to the modern western mindset. The understanding of these works place in the cannon of world literature is essential to an understanding of poetry, history, literature and the written word.

Major Works
Poems
The Iliad
The Odyssey

Dante (Durante Degli Alighieri)

*1265
†1321

Italian

The Devine Comedy was written in a new language which Dante called 'Italian', based on the regional Tuscan dialect. By creating a work of such epic structure and content he displayed a move away from Latin, increasing levels of literacy in Italy. He is guided through hell and purgatory by the Roman poet Virgil and then through Heaven by his lover, Beatrice. The poem is an exhibition of human life and moral instruction. It symbolises Dante's allusions on history, philosophy, astronomy, theology and science. His work was rediscovered in the 19th century by romantics, especially Blake, who saw it as being as essential as Homer's epic works.

Major Works
Poems
The Banquet (1304-07)
Monarchia (1312-13)
The New Life (1295)
The Divine Comedy (written in three parts, canticas, consisting of 33 cantos each 1308-21)
Inferno (Hell)
Purgatory
Paradise'

Epic Poet

John Milton

1608-1674
English

Considered the father of English poetry, a highly intelligent and studious man he used his vast talent for political, social and religious comment and analysis. His use of blank verse was extremely important to 18th century poetic progression and his treatment of issues such as the sublime, fate and the holy trinity was tremendously radical for its time. Milton addressed the important questions of his day but transgressed them in such a staggering way that his work is still relevant. His condemnation of the monarchy and his ideas on the church, which he saw as corrupt, are all addressed in his poetry and political writings. His greatest work, *Paradise Lost*, stands as one of the great works in English poetical verse and was composed by Milton for consumption by the common man.

Major Works
Poems
Comus (1634)
Lycidas (1638)
Paradise Lost
(1667 published in ten
books then in 1674 published
as twelve books)
Paradise Regained (1671)

Epic Poet and critic of Monarchy and Religion

Jonathan Swift

1667–
1745
Anglo-
Irish

Although a prominent and brilliant political essayist and commentator; he published the majority of his work anonymously and received little recognition until the 20th century. Funny and playful in its style but harshly critical and scathing of its targets his fictional work can be seen as a sophisticated satire of human nature based on his own experiences. His savagely satirical attacks would have been seen as severe in their political and religious overtones. His characterisation seduces the reader and enables the relvelations of the problems and injustices of Swift's time. His characterisation has come to be his most influential literary technique and the reason for his literary revival in the 1900's.

Major Works

Novels

The Battle of Books (1704)

A Tale of a Tub (1704)

Drapier's Letters (1724)

Gulliver's Travels (1726)

A Modest Proposal (1729)

Poems

Verses on the Death of Dr. Swift (1739)

'When a great genius appears in the world the dunces are all in confederacy against him'

Satire and Political Commentary

William Blake

1757– 1827

English

Blake never attended school or received any formal education; he was an engraver to the Society of Antiquities and was largely unrecognised in his lifetime. In his work, both poetry and his etchings, he felt the need to escape from the clutches of the 18th century versification as well as the materialist philosophy of the enlightenment and a puritanical or repressive interpretation of Christianity. He attempted to display the realities of his time and the struggle of the life of the common man through scathing satirical verse and philosophical interpretations of god and religion.

Major Works

Poems

Songs of Innocence and Experience (1794)

The Book of Thel (1789)

The Marriage of Heaven and Hell (1790-93)

Visions of the Daughters of Albion (1793)

The Book of Los (1795)

Jerusalem: The Emancipation of the Giant Albion (1804-20)

Pre Romantic visionary poet

Lord (George Gordon) Byron
(6th Baron Byron of Rochdale)

1758– 1824 English

Byron's works are only part of his importance, his life itself has come to be regarded as a continuation of his literary characterisation. Having many affairs, both homo and heterosexual, and an incestuous relationship with his cousin. He was a hereditary peer, a regional leader of Italy's revolutionary organisation and was in Greece to help fight the war of independence against the Ottoman's. All these aspects of his life are incorporated into his conception of the 'Byronic Hero' an idealised individual who is ultimately flawed. He left a legacy of inspiration, exaggeration and the romantic ideal of freedom of the soul and spirit.

Major Works
Poems
The Giaour (1813)

The Corsair (1814)

Hebrew Melodies (1815)

The Prisoner of Chillon (1816)

Manfred (1817)

Beppo (1818)

Childe Harold's Pilgrimage (1812-18)

Don Juan (1819-24)

Mazzeppa (1819)

Theory and Criticism
English Bards and Scotch Reviewers (1809)

Romantic / Satirist

William Wordsworth

1770–
1850

English

He wrote about nature and reality, about his experiences and recollections. He wanted a poetry of the 'language of real men'. A poetry of emotion which reflected the power and tranquillity of nature. A very close friend of Samuel Taylor Coleridge, with whom he wrote and published the lyric ballads, the text considered to have defined and begun the romantic period.

Major Works
Poems
Lyric Ballads - 1st edition (with Samuel Taylor Coleridge) (1798)
Lyric Ballads – 2nd edition (This edition contains the preface which is considered the seminal critical text in Romantic Literature) (1800)
Poems in Two Volumes (1807)
The Excursion (1814)
The Prelude (Posthumously 1850)

Romantic (Egotistical Sublime)

Jane Austen

1775–
1817
English

Mostly her works concern relations and relationships, detailing the complicated social and cultural structures of the landed gentry in the 18th and 19th centuries. Her satirical style is only noticeable through the graceful description and fastidious attention to detail which mark her writing style. Her depiction of the inequality of the sexes and her interest in the relationships between men and women has made her an important social critic of her time. Her writing style has been identified as satirical realism, displaying the irony and inequalities of her social standing within her time.

Major Works
Novels
Sense and Sensibility (1811)
Pride and Prejudice (1813)
Mansfield Park (1814)
Emma (1815)
Northanger Abbey
(Posthumously 1817)
Persuasion
(Posthumously 1817)

'One half of the world cannot understand the pleasures of the other'

Social Realist and historical detailer

Edgar Allan Poe

1809–
1849

American

Was one of the first people to attempt to make a living from writing thus ultimately lived a poor and hard existence somewhat mimicking the morose and melancholy themes of his work. He saw all didactic poetry as illegitimate because poetry should only exist in a sensory state. His focus on aesthetic principles led him to be considered the creator of the modern short story format with the crescendo of action being developed from the first instance of the story. Also credited with the creation of modern detective genre with his creation of the character of C Auguste Dupin.

Major Works

Short Stories

Tales of the Grotesque and Arabesque (Collection) (1840)
The Black Cat (1843)
The Fall of the House of Usher (1839)
Ligeia (1838)
The Masque of the Red Death (1842)
The Pit and the Pendulum (1842)
The Purloined Letter (1844)
The Tell Tale Heart (1843)

Poems

Annabel Lee (Posthumously 1849)
The City in the Sea (1845)
The Conqueror Worm (1843)
The Raven (1845)

Theory and Criticism

The Philosophy of Composition (1846)
Eureka: A Prose Poem (1843)
The Poetic Principle (1848)

Romanticism (Gothic)

Emily and Charlotte Bronte

1818-48
1816-55
English

Both sisters lived the vast majority of their lives in and around their home in Yorkshire. Charlotte was the more revered writer in her time. Passionately anti-Catholic her novels are praised for their depth of feeling and for their realism, especially in female / male interaction and her analysis of the subservient position of 19th century women in upper class society. Like Austin they were interested in the trivia of life but fiercely didactic. Emily was more romantic in her writing, *Wuthering Heights* was seen as morbid and violent but has come to be a seminal romantic text. The novel has a revolutionary structure and a complex narrative arrangement.

Major Works
Novels
Wuthering Heights (1847)
Emily (1847)
Jane Eyre (1847)
Shirley (1849)
Charlotte Villette (1853)

George Eliot (pseudonym for Mary Anne Evans)

1819–
1880
English

Like Austin she was a recorder of country life, although she did not simply record but politicised her work. She examined small town persecution and hypocrisy of gentry life. She sought to examine the mundane of ordinary life and display domestic realism through pathos and humour. Her novels contain deep psychological insight into her characters, especially female ones. She used her own personal refusal to attend church to examine alienation in society. Her examination of moral sensibility and her vast intelligence shine through in her work.

Major Works

Novels

Adam Bede (1859)
The Mill on the Floss (1860)
Silas Marner (1861)
Romola (1863)
Felix Holt, the Radical (1866)
Middlemarch (1871-72)
Daniel Deronda (1876)

*'Falsehood is so easy,
truth so difficult.'*

Realist and Social detailer

Herman Melville

1819–
1891
American

Born into poverty, at the age of twenty he became a cabin boy and for the next five years travelled around the world on whalers. Lived on the French Polynesian Islands, Tahiti and Honolulu. He then enlisted as a seaman in the United States navy. This part of his life provided the inspiration for the travel fiction for which he was famed during his early literary career. From 1866 he lived in obscurity as a New York customs agent, his popularity having completely faded after the confused text of *Pierre*. He has become regarded as a great stylist and realistic narrator, a shrewd social critic and philosopher.

Major Works
Novels
A Peep at Polynesian Life (1846)
Omoo: A Narrative of the Southern Sea (1847)
Mardi: A Voyage Thither (1849)
Redburn: His First Voyage (1849)
White-Jacket (1850)
Moby Dick (1851)
Pierre (1852)

The Confidence Man:
His Masquerade (1857)
Billy Budd (Posthumously 1924)

Short Stories
The Piazza Tales (1856)
Bartelby the Scrivener
Benito Careno
The Encantadas

Realist / Satirist

Fyodor (Mikhailovich) Dostoevsky

1821–1881

Russian

One of the greatest novelists of all time, his ability to mix all elements of the literary cannon has been an enormous influence and inspiration to a vast amount of writers and critics. His astounding character analysis was the vessel for the exploration of the human psychology of nineteenth century Russian society. This mixed with this depiction of the realities of Russian life developed the Russian novel and together with Tolstoy changed literature forever.

Major Works

Novels

Notes From the
Underground (1846)
Crime and Punishment (1866)
The Idiot (1869)
The Brothers Karamazov
(1880)

'To achieve perfection, one must first begin by not understanding many things'

Precursor to Twentieth Century existentialism

Gusstave Flaubert

1821–
1880

French

Amongst the most influential writers of modern times. It was Flaubert who created the modern aesthetic style and structure of the novel. Concerned with authenticity of detail, impersonal narrative and a precise and harmonious style. He concentrated on psychological development eradicating unnecessary detail and distractions in the construction of his characters and the words they inhabit. The composition of his text was extremely arduous as he sought to configure the truth through a prose compiled of the exact words, fitting together in harmonic perfection. This tended to mean his work would override moral and social issues in order to portray the truth exactly.

Major Works
Novels
Madame Bovary (1857)
Salammbo (1862)
Sentimental Education (1869)
Bouvard et Pecuchet
(Posthumously 1881)

Correspondence
Flaubert in Egypt:
A Sensibility on Tour (1972)

"The author in his work must be like god in the universe, present everywhere and visible nowhere."

Realist and Romantic

Leo (Nikolayevich) Tolstoy

1828–
1910
Russian

Although born into an aristocratic family he developed an anarchistic, Christian view point. Preaching non-violent resistance, the renunciation of wealth and the abolition of government and church.
His ideas were central to the philosophy of both Ghandi and Martin Luther King.
He is regarded as one of, if not the greatest, novelist of all time. He is a major influence on Joyce, Woolf, Flaubert and a vast number more. His depiction of the Napoleonic wars in War and Peace and of Russian life in Anna Karenina are revered as two of the greatest accomplishments in literary history. The realism, characterisation and narrative techniques blend history, fiction and socio-political commentary to create his masterful effect.

Major Works

Novels

Childhood, Boyhood and Youth (Respectively 1952, 54, 57 and collectively 1886)
The Cossacks: Tales from the Caucuses (1863)
War and Peace (1865-69)
Anna Karenina (1875-77)
The Death of Ivan Ilyitch and other stories (1887)

Hadji Murad (1904)

Theory and Criticism

The Kingdom of God is Within You (1894)
What is Art? (1898)

Realist and a precursor to anarchism.

Mark Twain
(pseudonym for Samuel Longhorn Clemens)

1835–
1910

American

Twain is considered the finest American author of the 19th century, if not of all time. The Adventures of Huck Finn is the classic American saga, Hemingway said of it that 'all modern American literature comes from one book by Mark Twain called Huck Finn'. His work is satirical and humorous but is ultimately a chronicle of the profane vanities, hypocrisies and denigrations of mankind. His work was able to not just present but induces in readers the experience of American life by combining frontier realism and western humour. However underlying the humour is a vigorous desire for social justice and a pervasive equalitarian attitude.

Major Works
Novels
The Prince and the Pauper (1882)
A Connecticut Yankee in King Arthur's Court (1889)
The Adventures of Tom Sawyer (1876)
The Adventures of Huckleberry Finn (1884)
The Tragedy of Pudd'nhead Wilson (1894)

'Always acknowledge a fault frankly. This will throw those in authority off their guard and give you opportunity to commit more.'

Satire and Humorist

Emile Zola

1840–
1902
French

The most prominent French novelist of the late 19th century, very important in the liberalisation of French society. In 1898 he risked life and career when he wrote a letter entitled 'Jaccuse' to a Parisian newspaper, structured as an open address to the President it accused the army of anti-semitism and obstruction of justice due to the wrongful conviction of a Jewish army general. The letter split France between army and church and liberal and commercial society. It is seen as the turning point of French power toward the intellectual, shaping the public, media and state. His work is inspired by heredity and environment to form social depictions of the relations of his characters and 19th century France.

Major Works

Les Rougon – Macquart
(1871-93 the twenty part saga depicting the natural and social history of Frances Second Empire, the reign of Napoleon the 3rd , through two families the Rougon's and the Marquart's)
Les Trois Villes (1894-98)
Les Quatre Evangiles
(1899-1902)

Naturalist

Knut Hamsun

1859–
1952
Norwegian

Born into poverty he worked as an itinerant labourer in Norway and America until settling back in Norway in 1898. An advocate of German culture he supported Germany in both world wars. He met with Hitler and wrote an obituary calling him a 'Warrior for mankind'. He was tried in Norway for his support of National Socialism but was acquitted when he was 88. He can be seen as one of the creators of the modern novel. His lyrical, abrupt and vivid prose concerned itself with the wandering protagonists or itinerant strangers. His novels depict nature and mankind united in a somewhat mystical bond. A commentator on the position of wealth and materialism and its juxtaposition by the realities of life and nature.

Major Works
Novels
Hunger (1880)
Mysteries (1892)
Pan (1894)
Victoria (1889)
Growth of the Soil (1917)
An Overgrown Pathos (1949)

Nobel Prize for Literature 1920

Realist and Social commentator

Marcel Proust

1871–1922

French

An isolated genius who spent the greater part of his writing life in isolation attempting to detail the human condition through new and inventive narrative techniques.

Major Works

Novels

Remembrance of Things Past (Published in seven parts from 1913-1927)

Swann's Way (1913)

Within a Budding Grove (1919)

The Guermantes Way (Published in two volumes 1920/21)

Sodom and Gomorrah (Published in two volumes 1921/22)

The Prisoner (1923)

The Fugitive (1925)

Past Recaptured (1927)

Pleasures and Regrets (1896)

James (Augustine Aloysius) Joyce

1882–
1941

Irish

Revolutionised the form and structure of the novel. Changed the way people saw communication and the development of language and characterisation.

Major Works
Novels
Dubliners (1914)
A portrait of the Artist as a young man (1916)
Ulysses (1922)
Finnegan's Wake (1939)

Modernist

Virginia Adeline Woolf

1882–
1941

English

Major literary figure in both modernist and feminist movements, changed the understanding of narrative techniques, pioneering stream of consciousness, and the development of characterisation.

Major Works

Novels
Jacob's Room (1922)
Mrs Dalloway (1925)
To the Lighthouse (1927)
Orlando: A Biography (1928)

Theory and Criticism
A Room of One's Own (1929)
Three Guineas (1938)

Modernist

Franz Kafka

1883–
1924
Czech

Considered to be one of the most influential writers of the 20th Century. His literary style incorporated existentialism, Marxism, anarchism and magical realism in an anti-capitalist perspective. His characterisation is the depiction of people in absurd, dehumanised positions; normally within a totalitarian society. His writing is hugely influenced by his own frail health and the fascist attitudes creeping into Prague, where he lived. Thus mental and physical collapse, alienation and persecution are essential themes to his work. His influence is essential to writers such as Marquez, Neruda and Rushdie as he showed them a way of presenting their ideals through the fantastical elements of reality.

Major Works
Novels
The Trial (1925)
The Castle (1926)
Amerika (1927)

Short Stories and Novellas
Metamorphosis (1915)
The Penal Colony: Stories and
Other Pieces (1948)
The Sons (1989)

'A book must be the axe for the frozen sea inside us.'

Modernism and Existentialism

(T)homas (S)tern Eliot

1888–
1965

English

Vital to an understanding of stream of consciousness, the lost generation and the modernist aesthetic.

Major Works

Poetry
Prufrock and other observations (1917)
Poems (1920)
The Wasteland (1922)
Journey of the Magi (1927)
The Hollow Man (1925)
Ash Wednesday (1930)
Four Quartets (1943)

Theory and Criticism
Tradition and the individual talent (1920)
The sacred wood: Essay's on poetry and criticism (1920)
The Frontiers of Criticism (1936)

Nobel Prize Winner (1948)

Modernist

(F)rancis Scott (Key) Fitzgerald

1896–
1940

American

Enlisted in the American army during World War One but the war ended before he saw action. The Great Gatsby can be seen as the quintessential novel of the literary period, dealing with Fitzgerald's coined 'Jazz Age', the Lost Generation and the idea of the American Dream.

Major Works

Novels

The Beautiful and the Damned (1922)
The Great Gatsby (1925)
Tender is the Night (1934)
The Last Tycoon
(Posthumously 1942)

Short Stories

Tales of the Jazz Age (1922)

Modernist

(Paul) Thomas Mann

1898– 1956

German

With the out brake of WWII Mann moved to Switzerland, later becoming a Cezch citizen in 1936. He then moved to America, not returning to Europe untill 1952. An essential literary pressence of the 20th Century he has been a major influence on subsequent generations of writers. Concerned with the nature of the artist; he constantly addressed the character and writer in relation to society. Also disscussed role of the artist in creating social institutions, such as Nazism.

Major Works
Novels
Buddenbrooks (1901)
The Magic Mountain (1924)
Joseph and His Brothers Tetralogy
The Tales of Jacob (1933)
The Young Joseph (1934)
Joseph in Egypt (1936)
Joseph the Provider (1943)
Dr. Faustus (1947)

Short Stories and Novellas
Tristan (1903)
Death in Venice (1912)
Tonio Kroger (1903)
Felix Krull (1922)
Theory and Criticism
Observations of an Unpolitical
Man (1918)

Nobel Prize for Literature 1929

Role of the Artist and the Bildungsroman

Jorge (Francisco Isidoro) Luis Borges (Acevedo)

1899–1986

Argentina

First Latin American writer to incorporate Magical Realism into their work. Combining the fantastical with the real he attempted to address complex topics which included the relationship between truth, fiction and identity. The cyclical nature of time and history is another major component of his writing. His stories are vast inter-changing visions which use dream like structures of interchanging magic and reality. Grounded in modernism but with a keen interest in existentialism and phenomenology he was a thinker of incredible esteem who changed Latin American literature paving the way for writers such as Marquez and Allende.

Major Works
Short Story Collections
A Universal History of Infamy
(1935)
The Garden of Forking Paths
(1941)
Ficciones (1944)
Artifices (1944)
The Aleph (1949)
Labyrinths (1962)
The Book of Sand (1975)

Magical Realist and Social Critic

Ernest (Miller) Hemingway

1899–1961

American

Member of the 1920's expatriate generation (the lost generation) who settled in Europe after the First World War. He fought in the Italian Infantry (1918) and travelled to Spain to report on their civil war (1937). He developed a journalistic, minimalist writing style that captured the modernist aesthetic in literary form. Particularly interested in the natural world and the primitive nuances of man.

Major Works

Novels

In Our Time (1925)
The Sun Also Rises/ Fiesta (1926)
A Farewell to Arms (1929)
Death in the Afternoon (1932)
For Whom the Bell Tolls (1940)

The Old Man and the Sea (1952)
A Moveable Feast
(Posthumously 1964)Islands in the
Stream (Posthumously 1970)

Short Stories

The Fifth Column and the First
Forty Nine Stories (1938)

Pulitzer Prize Winner – 1953
Nobel Prize Winner – 1954

Modernist

Vladimir (Vladimirovich) Nabokov

1899–
1977
Russian /
American

A man of vast intellectual ability who was a expert in both entomology and chess as well as one the most important writers in the second half of the twentieth century. A teacher and lecturer until the publication of *Lolita* made him a wealthy man he became a US citizen in 1945 only returning to Europe when he was able to sustain himself through writing. His early novels, written in Russian, are marked by their parody which he later transferred to his English novels. He developed a lyric style which used extraordinary descriptive and linguistic ability to infuse his novels with vivid description and thematic complexity. He influenced a whole generation of subsequent novelists.

Major Works

Novels:

King, Queen, Knave (1928)
Laughter in the Dark (1932)
Invitation to a Beheading (1938)
Bend Sinister (1947)
Lolita (1955)
Pnin (1957)
Pale Fire (1962)

'Lolita, light of my life, fire of my loins. My sin, my soul. Lo-lee-ta'

Modernist / Post-Modernist

John (Ernst) Steinbeck (Jr.)

1902–
1968

American

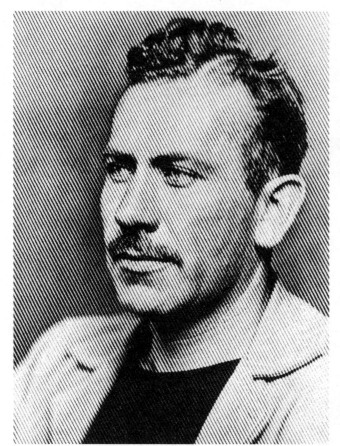

Lived in Small Frontier town and worked as a farm hand seeing the realities of migrant working life first hand. A champion of Americas poor, he chronicled the lives of the 1930's migrant population. Steinbeck depicted the validation of the anger and stoicism of the common man. He used realism to detail how greed and the labour market had destroyed the bond between nature and man. His work merges political realities and literary modernism as he celebrates rural communities and immigrant culture endorsing both conservative values and radical politics at the same time. *The Grapes of Wrath* presents a kaleidoscopic view of the history of the 1930's in California.

Major Works
Novels
Tortilla Flats (1935)
Of Mice and Men (1937)
The Grapes of Wrath (1939)
Cannery Row (1945)
The Pearl (1947)
East of Eden (1952)
The Winter of Our Discontent (1961)
Travels with Charley (1962)

'Unless a reviewer has the courage to give you unqualified praise, I say ignore the bastard.'

Pulitzer Prize in 1940

Nobel Prize for Literature 1962

Magical Realist and Social Critic

Pablo Neruda
(pseudonym for Neftali Ricardo Reyes Basoalto)

1904–1973 Chilean

A diplomat and government official for the majority of his life, his time working in Spain during the Spanish Civil War (1936-39) made him an ardent Marxist for life. A supporter of Salvador Allende he lived just long enough to see Chile's Marxist government be succeeded by Pinochet's coup. A poet of vast talent and scope his work ranges from experimental erotic love poems to committed work of a socialist agenda. In his life time he was one of the most prestigious leftwing intellectuals in the world. His work is experimental in its style shifting from surrealism to realism but from 1930's onward it is always politically and socially motivated. His *Canto General* is an important study of South American flora, fauna, history and detailing of indigenous peoples.

Major Works

Poetry

Twenty Love Poems and
a Desperate Song (1924)
Residence on Earth
(1933,35,47)
Canto General (15 sections
which are a combined history
of South America 1956)
One Hundred Love Sonnets
(1960)

Elementary Odes (1954-59)
Book of Questions (1974)
Isla Negra: A Notebook
(five volumes 1964)
Passions and Impressions
(1977)

Nobel Prize for Literature 1971

Surrealist, Realist and Social Critic

Albert Camus

1913–1968 French/ Algerian

Born in Algeria to French parents he was an actively committed socialist who opposed totalitarianism and capital punishment. He is cited with being a major force behind the existential-ist and absurdist move-ments, exploring the dual nature of reality, which he saw as being the absurd eg. happiness in the face of our impending mortality. Morality is a central theme to Camus work, the cause and effect that it has on everyday life. In his most acclaimed novels the protagonist exists juxtaposed to the societies they inhabit, this is done to display the failings of the socio-economic status quo. He was a huge philosophi-cal and literary influence who bridged the gap be-tween western and African literature in his attempts to identify the morality within the colonial mindset.

Major Works
Novels
The Stranger/The Outsider (1942)
The Plague (1947)
The Fall (1956)

Short Stories
Exile and Kingdom (1957)

Theory and Criticism
The Rebel (1951)

'Always go too far, because that's where you'll find the truth'

Nobel Prize for Literature 1957

Existentialist and Absurdist

Alexander (Isayevich) Solzhenitsyn

1918–2008 Russian / American

Born in the USSR he joined the Red Army in 1941, he was subsequently arrested in 1945 for anti-Stalinist remarks and spent the next seven years in a Gulag. He was released into exile in 1953. In 1956 he returned to Russia as a teacher. After the discovery of the Gulag Archipelago manuscript the Soviet government deported him to West Germany in 1974. He Settled in the United States in 1976 and lived there until his Russian citizenship was restored in 1990, he returned to Russia in 1994. Depicted the realism of Gulag life and offered a different perspective on Soviet history. A staunch critic of Stalin and Stalinist Russia he lived the life that he detailed in his novels, a loner battling against the hardship of the world.

<u>Major Works</u>
Novels
One Day in the Life
of Ivan Denisovich (1962)
Matrena's House (1963)
Cancer Ward (1968)
The First Circle (1969)
The Gulag Archipelago
(Three Volumes from 1973-75)
August 1914 (1971)

*Nobel Prize
for Literature in 1970.*

Realist and Social Critic

Primo (Michele) Levi

1919–1987

Italian

Italian Jewish chemist who was caught up in the Nazi occupation of northern Italy. Sent to Auschwitz in February 1944 he spent eleven months there before being liberated by the Red Army. His memoires of Auschwitz and his questioning of what it means to be human are essential to an understanding of the Holocaust. He was both an observant and objective witness applying the moral of 'forgive but don't forget'. His writing possess clarity of expression, ironic humour and metaphorical imagination. Added to his experiences this created formidable works identifying the nature of humanity.

Major Works

Novels
The Wrench (1987)
If Not Now, When? (1984)

Memoires
If This is Man (1947)
The Truce (1963)

Poems
Collected Poems (1975-84)

Short Stories
The Periodic Table (1975)

'A country is considered the more civilised the more the wisdom and efficiency of its laws hinder a weak man from becoming too weak and a powerful one too powerful.'

Holocaust, Historical and Science

Nadine Gordimer

1923

South African

Gordimer has lived in South Africa all her life; a staunch anti-apartheid activist and member of the ANC. Many of her books were banned by the South African government. An active critic and analyser of South Africa, its racial and social problems and the greater implications of colonial rule and pressure. Mostly her work is politically motivated or deeply concerned with political assessment. Always questioning power relations she portrays the themes of her work through the actions and choices of her characters.

Major Works

Novels
The Late Bourgeois World (1966)
The Conservationist (1974)
Burger's Daughter (1979)
July's People (1981)
The Pickup (2002)

Short Stories
The Soft Voice of the Serpent (1952)
Day's Footprint (1960)
Livingstone's Companions (1970)
Once Upon a Time (1989)

Booker Prize in 1974
(The Conservationist)
Nobel Prize for Literature 1991

Historical and Social Commentator

Günter (Wilhelm) Grass

1927

German

An active and committed socialist, his novels have become the literary spokesman for the German generation who grew up in the Nazi era and survived the war. His novels are concerned with a moral earnestness which may have come from him being in the Hitler Youth and being drafted, during the war, into the Waffen-SS at seventeen. He is important for his historical commentary and his inclusion of magical realist elements. His work is significant in his analysis of the post Nazi German mindset and social structure.

Major Works
Novels
The Danzig Trilogy:
The Tin Drum (1951)
Cat and Mouse (1961)
Dog Years (1963)

The Flounder (1977)
The Meeting at Telgate (1979)
The Rat (1986)
Crabwalk (2002)

Nobel Prize for Literature in 1999.

Socialist

Gabriel (Jose de la Concordia) Garcia Marquez

1927
Columbian

Part of the Latin American 'Boom' he is a politically motivated writer who's use of magic and satire to portray the socio-political situation of Latin America has become an essential aspect in understanding the modern mindset of South Americans. He mingles the ordinary with the miraculous in order to detail historical and social injustice, political wrongs and to depict the vivid colour and life of Latin America people. His work is a critic of post colonialism and colonial oppression which he sees as having an everlasting effect on Latin American life. His writing has become enormously influential to proceeding generations of novelists from around the world for its beautiful lilting style but also for its stinging presentation and discussion of social injustice.

Major Works

Novels

One Hundred Years of Solitude (1967)

The Autumn of the Patriarch (1975)

Chronicle of a Death Foretold (1981)

Love in the Time of Cholera (1988)

The General in his Labyrinth (1989)

Short Stories and Novellas

Leaf Storm (1955)

Strange Pilgrims (1993)

News of a Kidnapping (1996)

'A famous writer who wants to continue writing has to be constantly defending himself against fame. I don't really like to say this because it never sounds sincere, but I would really have liked for my books to have been published after my death, so I wouldn't have to go through all this business of fame and being a great writer'

Magical Realist and Social Critic

(Albert) Chinua (Iumogu) Achebe

1930

Nigerian

His novels detail the colonisation process, the Igbo culture of Nigeria proceeding colonial rule and pre colonial reality. His use of English in his writing is due to it being a unifying language; making it possible to communicate with the whole of the African continent. His books use oral traditions and a poetic style to convey racial, social and ideological problems of colonial rule and the depiction of the pre colonial African mindset. Achebe is interested in the religious aspects of colonialism, detailing the opposing ideas of Christianity and the actuality of a Western presence in Africa, comparing this to traditional African religious practices.

Major Works
Novels
Things Fall Apart (1958)
No Longer at Ease (1960)
Arrow of God (1964)
Man of the People (1966)
Anthills of the Savannah (1987)
Theory and Criticism
An Image of Africa: Racism in Conrad's 'Heart of Darkness' (1975)

'The white man is very clever. He came quietly with his religion. We were amused at his foolishness and allowed him to stay. Now he has won our brothers... He has put a knife on the things that held us together and we have fallen apart.'

Booker International Prize 2007

Post Colonial critic and analyst

(Sir) (V)idiadhar (S)urajprasad Naipaul

1932

British

A post colonial critic of serious significance; not only is his work hugely important in its depictions of socio-political factors but his precise and measured style presents a broad and melancholy view of human nature. His work concerns the Caribbean, India and Africa and seeks to present the reality of these places through strict structural techniques which at times can feel detached from the actuality of his characters.

Major Works
Novels
The Mystic Masseur (1957)
A House for Mister Biswas (1961)
The Mimic Men (1967)
In a Free State (1971)
Guerillas (1975)
A Bend in the River (1979)

Theory and Criticism
The Middle Passage (1962)
An Area of Darkness (1964)

Booker Prize in 1971
(In a Free State)

Nobel Prize for Literature 2001

Realist

(Sir) Salman (Ahmed) Rushdie

1947

Indian / British

His bio cultural upbringing informs all his work. He has shaped the form of Indo-Anglo writing and post colonial thought. His magical realist stories combine fantastical characterisation with historical realities to critic the Indian mindset and colonial rule. His vivid descriptions of food, colour and smell help to depict a world where cultural significance and colonial examination are mixed; presenting his view of modern India and post colonial societies in general.

Major Works

Novels
Midnights Children (1981)
Shame (1983)
The Satanic Verses (1988)
The Moor's Last Sigh (1995)
Shalimar the Clown (2005)

Theory and Criticism
The Jaguar Smile (1987)
Imaginary Homelands (1992)

'Literature is where I go to explore the highest and lowest places in human society and in the human spirit, where I hope to find not absolute truth but the truth of the tale, of the imagination of the heart.'

Booker Prize in 1981

Post Colonialism, Satire and Magical Relaism

Ben Okri

1959

Nigerian

Abandoning social and political themes of other African Writers work Okri seeks to combine western modernist narrative with the oral and spiritual traditions of African society. *The Famished Road* uses magical realism to represent the repetitive cycle of African oppression. Told through the Yoruba myth of an abiku, a baby of ambiguous existence destined to die and be reborn in a constant cycle. The book exists in the dream world of African tradition and the reality of the Nigerian civil war and colonial oppression.

Major Works
Novels
Flowers and Shadows (1980)
The Landscape Within (1981)
The Famished Road (1991)
Songs of Enchantment (1993)
Dangerous Love (1996)
Astonishing the Gods (1995)
In Arcadia (2002)

Booker Prize in 1991

Comedy / Satire

Chapter 6.
Drama Introduction

Top Ten PLays

"Waiting for Godot" by Samuel Beckett.
"Antigone" by Sophocles.
"The Tempest" by Shakespeare.
"Hedda Gabbler" by Ibsen.
"The Importance of Being Earnest"
by Oscar Wilde
"Death of a Salesman" by Arthur Miller.
"Marat/Sade: as performed by the Inmates of
Charanton" by Peter Weiss.
"The Maids" by Jean Genet.
"The Trojan war will not take place"
by Girodoux.
"Rinocherous" by Ionesco.

The study of plays poses two main questions; what is the written words purpose, and what should the piece aesthetically look like? The latter question distinguishes between the study of a novel and the study of a play.

Drama is written to be produced and performed; it is a physical process that relies on action and the reaction of an observer/ audience. Modern theatres are reminiscent of the ancient Greek model of an amphitheatre, separating actor and audience. Although this has continued to be a popular way to stage drama, playwrights have created performance spaces to reflect the tension and emotion in their narrative. When studying the creation and production of drama it is important to acknowledge the physical aspects of a play, identifying the playwrights desire to create a spectacle. The play, unlike the novel has a physical presence of its own, one that changes with every performance and every cast.

Playwrights Timeline of Dramatic movements

Ancient Theatre:
Sophocles

Medieval Theatre:
Anonymous writers;
Everyman, Mankind

Restoration:
Aphra Behn

Eighteenth Century:
Richard Brinsley Sheridan

European Classics and
Romanticism;
Johann Wolfgang Goethe

Early Modern:
Ben Johnson, Shakespeare

Victorian and Melodrama:
Colin H Hazelwood

19th Century and
Naturalism:
Anton Chekhov
Henrik Ibsen

Modern European:
Samuel Beckett
Bertolt Brecht

Twentieth Century British;
Harold Pinter
Caryl Churchill

Twentieth Century American;
Author Miller
Tennessee Williams

William Shakespeare

*1564–
†1616

British

Considered the father of Theatre. Wrote 154 sonnets, two long poems, a collection of short poems and 38 plays. Influencing all that came after; his plays have been translated into every major language. The Romantics favoured Shakespeare for his use of beauty and nature and the Victorians re-established his plays' return to the theatre. He wrote in three main genres: comedies, tragedies and histories although towards the end of his career he wrote tragicomedies or romances such as *The Tempest*.

Major Works

Plays:

Midsummer's Night Dream (1595/96)
Romeo and Juliet (1594/95)
Richard III (1592/93)
Merchant of Venice (1596/97)
Hamlet (1600/01)
Richard II (1595/96)
Much Ado about Nothing (1598/99)

Othello (1604/05)
Henry V (1598/99)
The Tempest (1611/12)
Macbeth (1605/06)
Henry VIII (1613)

Poems:

Venus and Adonis
A Lovers Complaint
The Passionate Pilgrim

Christopher Marlow

1564–1593

British

Poet, dramatist and translator, contemporary of Shakespeare's. Murdered aged 29 he had only written and produced *Tamburlaine* and (II) when he died. Most notable work, his translation of *Faustbach* from German in which he changed the ending to include his protagonist being torn apart by daemons. *The Jew of Malta* is said to have influenced Shakespeare's *The Merchant of Venice*.

Major Works
Plays:
The Jew of Malta (posthumously 1633)
The Tragical History of Dr. Faustus (posthumously 1604)
Tamburlaine (1587)
Tamburlaine II (1590)

(Jean-Baptiste Poquelin) Moliere

1622–
1673

French

Comic writer and actor who used Moliere as his stage name. Took influence from Italian improvisational theatre; Commedia dell'Arte. Very influential in French culture, like Shakespeare, creating many new words for the French language. Mainly appreciated posthumously.

<u>Major Works</u>
<u>Plays</u>:
Tartuffe (1664)
The Misanthrope (1666)

Henrik Ibsen

1828–1906

Norwegian

Born into a wealthy Norwegian family who lost all their money. Ibsen's writing was greatly influenced by his own upbringing. He is considered the father of modern theatre and the creator of the 'Prose Play'. Through Ibsen's work European theatre became politically coherent. The exploration of the sub-conscious through dramatic irony explored the public and private personas of the ruling-class and became a post-Ibsen trait of play writing.

Major Works
Plays
Brand (1866)
Peer Gynt (1867)
Ghosts (1881)
AN Enemy of the People (1882)
Hedda Gabler (1890)
When we dead awaken (1899)

Realist / Naturalist

(Johan) August Strindberg

1849–
1912

Swedish

Educated in a middle-class private school before going to Uppsala University and failing to graduate, Strindberg found it difficult to commit to a career. He was greatly influenced by Ibsen, Hans Christian Anderson and Nietzsche which led him to an Expressionist style of theatre. Concentrating on emotional rather than physical naturalism would greatly influence The Theatre of the Absurd in the 20th century.

Major Works

Plays:
Master Olof (1872)
The Father (1887)
Miss Julie (1888)
The Death Dance (1900)
A Dream Play (1901)
Hellas (1903)
The Ghost Sonata (1907)

Novel/ Autobiography:
The Red Room (1879)
Son of Servand I-V (1886-1909)
Inferno (1897)

Naturalist / Expressionist

Oscar (Fingal O'Flahertie Wills) Wilde

1854– 1900
Irish

Educated at home until he was nine, by his mother who was a poet and an Irish Nationalist, Wilde went on to Portia Royal Boarding School and attended Trinity College Dublin and Oxford to study Classics. Wilde is still prevalent on drama courses due to the continuing success of *The Importance of Being Earnest*. His involvement in the aesthetic movement encouraged accusations of homosexuality leading to his imprisonment and subsequent refusal to return to the theatre. Wilde's concentration on the visual rather than moral or social issues pre-empted modernism.

Major Works

Plays
The Dutchess of Padua (1883)
Lady Windermere's Fan (1892)
The Importance of
being Earnest (1895)

Novels
The Picture of Dorian Gray
(1890)
Teleny or, The Reverse of the
Medal (1893)

Short Stories:
The Canterville Ghost (1887)

Aestheticism

George Bernard Shaw

1856–1950

Irish

Shaw attended various Grammar and Public schools in Ireland but saw education as stifling to his creativity. He was influential to British theatre and modern playwrights, believing that theatre in Britain was artificial. He demanded plays to be written to challenge social injustice rather than fuel it. Shaw called for the political deconstruction of society on the British stage to emulate the works of Ibsen and Strindberg in Scandinavia. He can be credited with bringing Naturalism to British theatre relying on real objects on stage to suggest a naturalist setting.

<u>Major Works</u>
<u>Plays</u>:
The Philanderer (1893)
The Devils Disciple (1897)
Caesar and Cleopatra (1898)
Man and Superman (1903)
Major Barbara (1905)
Pygmalion (1912-13)
Heartbreak House (1919)
Saint Joan (1923)

Nobel Prize for Literature 1925

Oscar (Pygmalion Film) 1938

Early Naturalism

Anton Checkhov

1860–
1904

Russian

Four later plays became central to the development of Naturalism within theatre both in Russia and Europe. His collaborations with Stanislavski's Moscow Art Theatre and its 1898 staging of *The Seagull* introduced a focus on the ensemble cast. Chekhov's political intentions and Stanislavski's use of a naturalistic setting have ensured the reproduction of his plays since his death in 1904.

Major Works
Plays:
Ivanov (1887)
The Seagull (1895)
Uncle Vanya (1900)
Three Sisters (1901)
The Cherry Orchard (1904)

Naturalist

Constantine Stanislavski

1863–1938

Russian

Stanislavski was the first theatre practitioner to create a 'system' for acting. Influenced by the Great Russian authors (Tolstoy, Gogol) he created Realism for the theatre; removed theatre from the Aristotelian model and concentrated on an ensemble cast that would convey real life through movement rather than through prose. He was a contemporary of Chekov and an unrivalled influence on the teachings of Naturalism in the theatre.

Major Works
Plays:
An Actor's Work:
A Student's Diary
My life in Art (1924)

Realism

Frank Wedekind

1864–
1918

German

Aliened with the early Expressionist movement, Wedekind is said to have had a great influence on Bertolt Brecht. His plays strove to express the emotional experiences of life rather than project a physical reality. His exploration of pubescent sexuality and social mobility is most clearly defined in *Lulu*. The rise and subsequent demise of a female protagonist demonstrates social decline due to infidelity and sexual exploration.

<u>Major Works</u>
<u>Plays</u>:
Spring Awakening (1891)
Earth Spirit (1895)
Lulu/ Pandora's Box (1904)

Expressionist

Antonin Artaud

1896-
1948
French

Contracted meningitis as a child which led to a period committed to a Sanatorium where he read widely: Rimbaud, Baudelaire and Edgar Allan Poe. Artaud also became dependant on opium based painkillers in his teens which returned throughout his life. Born from a rejection of Surrealism Artaud's Theatre of Cruelty reduced words and expressions into movements and sounds. He believed that the theatre could be more than a bourgeoisie art form and that by breaking the illusion between stage and audience the theatre could become influential. His influence on modern theatre is infinite which places him central to the study of drama.

Major Works
Manifesto:
The Theatre and It's Double
(1938)
Revised: (1958)

Theatre of Cruelty

J.B. Priestley

1894–
1984

British

Priestley served as a WWI infantry soldier before returning to Cambridge University and subsequently moving to London to become a journalist. His most famous plays had a preoccupation with time that was influenced by J.W. Dunne's: *Theory of Time.* The rejection of a linear narrative allowed Priestley to use dramatic irony throughout his plays as a narrative tool. The socialist sentiment of Priestley's plays lead to their description as a 'modern morality' play.

Major Works
Plays:
Dangerous Corner (1932)
I have Been here Before (1937)
Time and the Conways (1937)
An Inspector Calls (1946)
Novels:
The Good Companions (1929)
Angel Pavement (1930)
Bright Day (1946)
Lost Empires (1965)

Time Play / Socialist

(Eugen) Bertolt (Friedrich) Brecht

1898–1956

German

Most successful period of writing during exile from Hitler's Germany in 1941. Brecht is best known for his work with the Berliner Ensemble developing his style of didactic (instructive) theatre. A committed Marxist; he produced a system making the theatre a political forum. He believed if the audience were aware of the falsity of their surroundings then they would have a rational and critical analysis of the play. He has left a legacy of Brechtian playwrights and revolutionised modern theatre.

Major Works
Plays
The Life of Galileo (1939-43)
The Good Woman of Setzuan (1938-41)
Mother Courage (1941)
The Caucasian Chalk Circle (1948)

Modernist

Noel Coward

1899–
1973

British

Coward became one of Britain's wealthiest playwrights during WWII and had continuing success producing plays that depicted the lives of his contemporaries. His rejection of Beckett's use of symbolism and Osborne's `Kitchen Sink Drama´ established his theatre as escapism. Postmodern abstract theatre dismissed Cowards' theatrical techniques and his positive depiction of the ruling classes.

Major Works
Plays:
Fallen Angels (1925)
The Vortex (1924)
Hay Fever (1925)
Easy Virtue (1925)
Design For Living (1933)
Present Laughter (1939)
This Happy Breed (1939)
Blithe Spirit (1939)
Operette (musical Play) (1937)

Comedy / Satire

Samuel Becket

**1906–
1986
Irish**

Educated at the Portora Royal Boarding School and Trinity College Dublin. After graduating Becket lectured at Ecole Normale Superievure in Paris where he met and become close friends with James Joyce. Becket's literary influence is overshadowed by his theatrical. He distanced himself from a popular realist movement and instead focused on the human condition removing the burden of a linear narrative. His plays explore a modernist, post-modernist and absurd theatrical structure. This removal from one particular style meant *Waiting for Godot* becoming a seminal 20th century play replacing prose with motif and minimal language.

Major Works
Plays:
Eleutheria (1940)
Happy Days (1960)
Not I (1972)
Catastrophe (1982)
Novels:
Murphy (1938)
Malloy (1951)
Malone (1951)

Non-Fiction:
Proust (1931)

*Nobel Prize for Literature
(1969)*

Modernist / Post Modernist / Absurdity

John (James) Osborne

Osborne's first play Look Back in Anger won him critical acclaim after Kenneth Tynan's review of its showing at The Royal Court Theatre in 1956. His 'Kitchen Sink Drama' became the antithesis of Victorian 'Drawing Room Drama's' and a rebellion from a bourgeoisie representation of the upper class. George Fearon labelled Osborne one of the new generation of 'Angry Young Men', *Look Back in Anger* altered British post war theatre.

Major Works
Plays:
Look Back in Anger (1956)
The Entertainer (1957)
Epitaph for George Dillon (1957)
Hedda Gabler (adaptation)
(1972)
The Picture of Dorian Gray
(adaptation) (1975)
The Father (adaptation) (1989)

Postmodernist

Harold Pinter

**1930–
2008**

British

Poet playwright and director, his experiences of isolation, separation and abandonment as an evacuee inspired his work. Originally considered part of the Theatre of the Absurd, Pinter's plays have become seen as a 'Theatre of Menace'; in which contradictions of both good and bad are presented through each character. The term 'Pinteresque' is used by critics as a term to suggest the use of colloquial speech, exaggerated pauses and periods of silence to create meaning. Pinter himself rejected the definitions of his work referring to them as 'meaningless'.

<u>Major Works</u>
<u>Plays</u>:
The Room (1957)
The Birthday Party (1957)
The Caretaker (1959)
Tea Party (1964)
The Homecoming (1964)
No Man's Land (1974)   *Nobel Prize for Literature*
Betrayal (1978)   *2005*

Edward Bond

Bond left school early without gaining any formal qualifications. A working-class upbringing fuelled his political beliefs and inspired his playwriting. Invited to join the Royal Court's first 'writers group' in 1958 this led to the production of his first play *The Pope's Wedding*. *Saved* became the last play to be banned by the Lord Chamberlin's Men , overturned due to the defiance of the Royal Court Theatre. Bond's use of violence and sexuality has encouraged a title of a modern tragedian.

<u>Major Works</u>
<u>Plays</u>:
The Pope's Wedding (1962)
Saved (1965)
Early Morning (1967)
Narrow Road to the Deep North (1968)
Lear (1971)
Spring Awakening (1974)
The Sea (1973)
Bingo (1974)

Postmodernism

Caryl Churchill

1938–

British

Influenced greatly by Artaud, Strindberg and Brecht, Churchill's plays have feminist themes whilst using Expressionist and Absurdist visual imagery. After studying English Literature at Oxford University Churchill had already begun developing the exploration of assigned gender roles within her early works. Her collaborations with theatre groups such as Joint Stock and Monsterous Regiment allowed her to express her political interpretation on a theatrical stage. Her use of language and action shocked her audiences confronting them didactically rather than allowing them to be complacent in their observations.

Major Works
Plays:
Vinegar Tom (1976)
The After Dinner Joke (television) (1978)
Cloud Nine (1979)
Top Girls (1982)
Serious Money (1987)
A Dream Play (translation) (2005)
Drunk Enough to say I Love You (2006)

Postmodern Feminist

Sarah Kane

1971–
1999

British

Kane's plays focus on love, pain and suffering. A preoccupation with death and torture made her plays the most controversial since Edward Bond's *Saved*. Influenced by Beckett, Bond and Artaud, she won acclaim from Pinter and Churchill. Suffering from depression and psychosis she committed suicide aged 29.

Major Works
Plays:
Blasted (1995)
Phaedra's Love (1996)
Cleansed (1998)
4.48 Psychosis
(performed 2000)
Television:
Skin (1995)

Postmodern (In-Yer-Face)

Chapter 7.
History

'History is now strictly organized, powerfully disciplined, but it possesses only a modest educational value and even less conscious social purpose.' J. H. Plumb

The study of History

The study of history is one of the oldest academic pursuits but it is also one of the most fractious and contested areas of study. The main reason for the vast array of historical opinion and argument is due to the questioning of the nature of history itself. Who creates history? Who documents what is happening? For what end is history created? What is fact and what is fiction? These questions and questions like them are essential to the field of historical study at degree level. History at A-level is basically a discussion of a topic, using a textbook, which is taken for granted as facts based on primary evidence and correct scholarly interpretation. The idea of questioning all aspects of the historical interpretation with which you are presented is not considered as important as the ability to regurgitate 'fact'. This is the major difference between an A-level and degree level learning of history; in your degree you have the opportunity to understand that what we think constitutes as history, is open to all types of interpretation and analysis.

A Start to Western Historical Study

For the vast majority of us the historical interpretation we are familiar and comfortable with is that of western historical practices and theories. The person credited with creating this western historical viewpoint is the Greek writer and thinker Herodotus. Living between 484 and 425 BCE Herodotus has been called both the 'Father of History' and the 'Father of Lies'. His association with the start of historical study is due to his recordings of the conflict between Greece and Persia and the title which he gave this piece; *Historie* meaning inquiry in Latin. Herodotus' recordings are accepted as having given rise to a more systematic approach in the field of recording and interpreting past events.

Thucydides is another Greek thinker and recorder who was associated with revolutionising of history. Alive at the same time as Herodotus, Thucydides is regarded as the 'Father of Scientific History', for his various musings on the causes and effects of humanity. He is also known as the 'Father of Social Realism' due to his notion that relations between nations were based on might rather than right, a notion that rings as true in the modern world as it did when he was analysing nation state interactions over 400 years before the birth of Christ.

In terms of their impact on the field of historical study the Roman historian Tacitus was essential to the following generation's interpretation of history. His two great works *Annals* and *Histories* Tacitus attempted to examine the Roman Empire between the years 14 to 96 AD. His famous declaration about the bias of the historical recorder 'Hence my purpose is to relate... without either anger or veal, from any motive from which I am far removed' became a mantra for the impartiality of the western historian's judgement.

'History is a science, no more and no less.'
J. B. Bury

Four Fields of Historical Endeavour

1. History offers an insight and lessons which arise from the historical record itself.

From the start of the renaissance, in the 1400s, to the end of 18th Century history was taught by example. The ancient Greeks and Romans were exemplified as the essential models of morality and justice, their vices and virtues held up as lessons to subsequent generations. The fundamental problem with this approach is that for it to be of any use in terms of historical interpretation it must be assumed that the conditions of life now are the same as they were then and that as a result social and cultural comparisons can be made. This is, of course, a false notion which oversimplifies the changes which occur from era to era. Similar problems arise when the concept of the cyclical nature of history is discussed. Major events which seem to repeat themselves, such as revolutions and economic slumps, are dependent on much wider socio-economic factors and not simply due to some predestined cycle. Therefore this view relies on predictions made about future events on the evidence of past events which is history based on guess work. The lesson which this perspective of history can teach us is that we should not make firm assumptions about the world around us.

2. The discovery of what occurred and what it was like in the past.

In the beginning of the 19th Century, historicism was invented, in turn starting the modern recognised profession of historian. Led by men such as the German intellectual Leopold Von Ranke historicism emphasised the 'otherness' of the past due to it being fundamentally different from the present. This source based study was centred on two key components, the rigorous examination of primary texts and sources and empathy with the people of the past. This field of study saw the examination of primary evidence as essential to an understanding of any historical event, without a rigorous assessment of evidence directly from the time how were any conclusions meant to be drawn about a historical topic. The essential problem with such specific notions is that in examining the primary information the reasons for its creation are waylaid in order to discover the information which it contains. The socio-economic factors that go to creating a piece of evidence are not seen as important as the information which the piece of evidence contains.

Leopold Van Ranke
Von Ranke was a German historian writing in the 19th Century and is considered one of the founders of modern source based history. He introduced empiricism, an emphasis on narrative history and international politics. He thought that history should embrace the principle of 'Wie es eigentlich gewesen ist' (to show what essentially happened). We should judge history on source based material from the time and not as inferior or superior to periods before and after it.

3. The uncovering of the shape of human destiny through the patterns and purpose of history.

Initially a Christian view of history was prominent in western society but, with the enlightenment in the 18th Century came a perspective which saw history as a record of moral and material improvement.
This view of history, as a record of improvement, sees each subsequent generation as a progression of the previous one; however the belief in continuous progress has been one of the casualties of the 20th Century, resulting in two world wars, nuclear threat and environmental destruction.
The 19th Century also gave birth to Marxism which sees history in four clear stages, ancient, feudal, capitalist and socialist, each era more progressive than the last. Marxism sees everything through the medium of class and in relation to history the main focal points are that economic life is the benchmark for success and that progressive change can only come out of revolutionary conflict. Marx saw the move from feudalism to capitalism as the central change in modern times, exemplified by the French revolution in 1789. He argued that all major political changes have come through tensions in the socio-economic order.

4. Legitimising political institutions, leaders and glorifying nation states.

During the middle ages, roughly the 5th century to the start of the Renaissance, European States encouraged their scholars to embellish histories of their heroes, saints and leaders. These histories traditionally boasted superiority, internal order and support for the status quo. The men that created these 'histories' embellished the traditional memories of the people, exaggerating myths and tales that were already present and imbedded in the society's folk laws and traditions. The reason for these created histories was due to a perceived need to reinforce the superiority or control of a certain nation. In the 19th Century historians were again under pressure to credit the heroic and tragic elements of their society's popular culture. Young states or states with shifting political forums had more need to control the legitimacy of their histories, America's Western emancipation and Nazi Germany's Arian lineage. This creation of history in order to serve political means demonstrates the ability of history to serve any purpose for which is needed, simply by adopting the right interpretational manner.

What is History?

In his 1961 book *What is History?* the British historian E.H. Carr examined the field of historiography, looking at the creation of history and the use of historical methods. Primarily Carr was attempting to justify his argument that history's academic place lay not in the humanities but among the social sciences. Carr was presenting a way between the empirical view of historians such as Leopold Van Ranke and the idealist view of historians such as R.G. Collingwood. Collingwood saw history as the recollections of the lives and decisions of individuals, he did not consider facts of class, politics and gender as always affecting the perspective of the recorder. In the same vain as Von Ranke he thought that primary material on individuals was the proper way to study history. Carr completely rejected this idea; he said that 'before you study the history, study the historian' as it is he that determines which aspects of the past to turn into historical fact.

He said that the individual is almost void of direct historical influence and that focusing on them is to do an injustice to the past, historical institutions not individuals are what should be judged. Carr's famous explanation of his view of history is the reversal of a quote by the 20th Century historian George Clark. Clark said that history was a hardcore of fact surrounded by a pulp of interpretation whereas Carr saw it as 'A hardcore of interpretation surrounded by a pulp of disputable facts'. The Determinist view of history argues that all things have a cause and we should examine the events of the past in terms of all possible outcomes of that event, only then can we see the actuality of the situation that occurred. Carr dismissed this, he said that there are no accidents in history and therefore no need to examine possible outcomes as the actual outcome was the only realistic possibility. Carr saw it as being anti-historical to cast moral judgements in historical endeavours. Judging people from the past by the moral standards of the present was counterproductive and naive. He saw history as a means to progress humanity and that this progress was the main function of the historian.

Social Science or Humanities

Since the era of Enlightenment there has been contention between those who would group history as part of the humanities or as part of the social sciences. Is it a field of intrinsic enrichment or the key to understanding society and planning social change? The historicist tradition within history places history firmly within the humanities where as those who seek the relevance of history group it, with sociology and economics, as a social science. The essential difference is that where as the empirical approach to science studies primary evidence and the deeds of individuals, a social scientific approach assesses the more long term trends and attempts to draw comparisons without generalising. Although the traditional approach to history, in the western sense, is to examine fact and make judgment based on those facts the modern influences on historical study steer it toward a social science perspective where all aspects of an historical situation must be analysed before any judgments can be made.

Self Questioning and Reappraisal

With the coming of Post Modernism in the 1960s and the theories it brought with it the study of history dramatically changed. Post modernism sees language as constructing experience and not something that reflects, and then conveys the truth about, reality. What this means is that all aspects of language, verbal or written, are determined by cultural context and inclination of the reader. Therefore in terms of historical study all the historian can hope for is to place their work, constructively, within an appropriate field of study. The historian Michel Foucault developed a theory of power and knowledge which understands dominant discourses of truth as powerful constructs of the social world. We understand the world discursively through competing versions of its truth. The modern practice of history is seen as something to endow our lives with meaning but what comes out of so many schools of historical scholarship is that nothing can be known with any certainty.

Since the 1960s and 70s historical study in the west has changed drastically due to the rise in the importance of previously considered groups such as ethnic minorities and women. These minority groups have become prominent social and cultural critics and as a result have developed an identity based history which has contradicted much of what was thought to be previously true. To gain political power groups must first deconstruct the view of them held by the general public. A major aspect of that deconstruction is through the creation of specific historical viewpoints which counteract the stereotypical or false perceptions that have been created by historians who have not considered the socio-political impact of certain events on minority groups. These new perspectives in the field of historical study have changed the face of the discipline, making people perceive history with more of a social and political focus.

The French Historian Fernand Braudel, completely rejected the empirical school of history and encouraged a large scale socio-economic making and telling of history.

Essentially our European history is that of the powerful western structures of social, economic and cultural control. He saw neglected and minority groups as the essential aspects of understanding history.

The rise of a Post Colonial academic discipline has meant that a history which highlights the control and subservience of colonial presences objects to much of mainstream history. It has attempted to display the negative effects of colonialism and the damage to the culture and history of those colonised countries.

What has occurred since the rise in the prominence of minority and post colonial history is that western historical doctrines have come under huge pressure to identify and rectify their short comings. There is now recognition that much of the culturally embedded history of the west's past is constructed by, and from the perspective of, white men. This has been done in order to bolster the power and control of European societies and their superiority over countries which came under colonial control.

Conclusion

The field of historical study is an area that is constantly changing and adapting to new theories and perceptions. It has changed vastly over the two thousand years since Herodotus and has become a reflection of the shifting paradigms of twenty first century socio-economics. No longer are the definite pronunciations of old white men in Oxbridge's ivory towers the be all and end all of historical discussion. The field of Historical study was eloquently summed up by the polish historian Ihor Sevcenko when he likened it to a dog entering a virgin forest. The dog picks any tree at random and pees on it, despite the tree having no intrinsic attraction other dogs entering the forest show an overwhelming tendency to pee against the same tree. What Sevcenko is alluding to is that historians will attempt to analyse the same small parts of history, not for the progression of knowledge but due to some need for recognition and appraisal.

Since the introduction of post modernism and post colonialism the nature of our history in the west has come under severe scrutiny and for just reasons. Hopefully these two areas of study have made us question the nature of all historical 'fact' and have shown us that, in the words of the historian John Tosh, perspective, rather than prophecy, is the contribution historians can make to the rational understanding of the contemporary world.

Historical Principles

These are the essential questions that you need to ask yourself when assessing historical material.

Higher Criticisms

Who? – Date

Where? – Localisation

External Criticism

Whom? - Authorship

What Sources were used? - Analysis

Lower Criticism

What form was it produced in? – Integrity

Internal Criticism

Value of its content? – Credibility

Conflicting Historical Issues

Quantify the past or illuminate the modern world.

Passionless detachment or sympathetic engagement with peoples of the past.

About dates and deeds or how they represented and constructed their lives.

About individuals or evolution of society.

The importance of history is to carry arguments to a public forum without condescension and with a focus on accessibility.

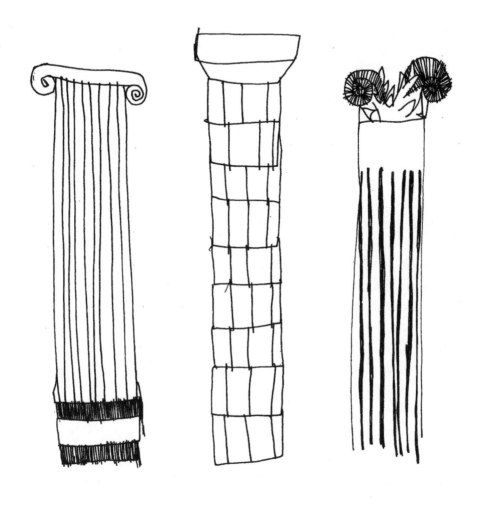

'Any fool can make history, but it takes
a genius to write it.' Oscar Wilde

Chapter 8.
Politics/Sociology

Everyone needs a basic grasp of the big questions, like what is democracy? How does society function? What is the point of education and are women equal to men? Whatever course you are doing at university it is important to have a grasp of the general cultural debate, the major theoretical aspects of world politics and trends and a rough idea of who the big thinkers are. There are, of course, endlessly complicated questions about the Enlightenment, reason and contemporary digital culture but without a basic grasp of the wider historical and theoretical debates it is easy to feel confused about making any kind of statement. This is a basic package of key people and ideas to get you through.

'Academic sociologists have been trained to conceive of their discipline -sociology- as the scientific study of society, and to remit to the sister discipline of psychology the study of individuals'. Richard Wall

'If voting changed anything, they'd make it illegal'. Emma Goldman (anarchist)

Individualism
The idea that the free, rational individual is at the centre of all political decision making. A modern theory that is much contested.

Marxism/Communism
The idea that everything must be done collectively, and that the working-classes are the future of mankind. Not very popular these days.

Conservatism
The idea that rich elites should rule everything because, by getting rich, they have proved that they are superior and therefore should run everything. Linked to Monarchy and tradition.

Social contract theory
The idea that somewhere there exists a contract between members of a society that regulates what they should do. Like all contracts this can be broken if you have a good lawyer.

Realism
The idea that most people are nasty and try and get power and wealth by any means possible, clearly not true.

Anarchism
Rejects all authority and believes in self-organisation, less collectivist than Marxism and prone to Individualism.

Pluralism
The idea that power is spread across different groups in society and that they compete on an equal basis.

Feminism
The idea that historically society has been patriarchal (run by men for men)and that a fundamental critique of society is necessary.

Elitism
The idea that there are natural elites in society who should run things (linked to Conservatism) goes back to Plato.

'The Top Twelve' Sociologists in History

Auguste Comte (1798-1857). French founder of 'Positivism', a doctrine that advocated a scientific method based on generalisations from observable phenomena and the application of that method to society; hence his invention of the term 'sociology', the 'science' of society. Basically looks at the structures and patterns of organisation of society.

Herbert Spencer (1820-1903). English polymath who applied a biological theory of evolution to philosophy and sociology. Like Comte, he often described society as an organism as a way of emphasising the interdependence of different human activities (the 'organic' view). Anticipated modern 'socio-biology'. Some of his ideas over-lapped with 'social-darwinism' – the idea of the survival of the fittest groups.

Charles Booth (1840-1916). English social investigator who pioneered the social survey method, by leading a group of investigators in his lengthy (multi-volume) study of poverty in London; *Life and Labour of the People of London* (1891-1903).

Emile Durkheim (1858-1917). By 1900, sociology had become a 'respectable' academic subject and Durkheim was one of its first university professors in France. In works such as *Suicide* (1897) and *The Elementary Forms of Religious Life* (1912), he argued that the scientific/organic approach of Comte and Spencer could even be applied to the most intensely personal of human decisions.

Clara Collet (1860-1948). English social investigator and collaborator of Charles Booth. A fellow empiricist, she made the first systematic study of women's employment (in East London) and wrote several notable essays on women's education.

Max Weber (1864-1920). German academic and the most individualistic of the four 'founding fathers' of sociology (Comte/Spencer/Durkheim/Weber). Applied rationalist ideas to the study of classes and institutions (theory of bureaucracy) but recognised the role of irrational emotions in political life (the idea of charisma).

Elsie Clews (1875-1941). American professor of anthropology, who is often considered to be the first feminist sociologist. Her first book, *The Family* (1903), included a long discussion of betrothal and trial marriage, while *The Old-Fashioned Woman* (1913) developed an unorthodox and critical analysis of traditional gender roles.

Karl Mannheim (1893-1947). The 'founding father' of the sub-discipline known as 'sociology of knowledge'. Distinguished between 'particular' and 'total' ideologies, the former referring to specific factual distortions, and the latter to certain intellectual views associated with specific social positions e.g. stockbrokers and entrepreneurs tend to favour free-market capitalism!

Talcott Parsons (1902-1979). American founder of the 'structural-functionalist' or 'action theory' school of sociology. Attempted to synthesise the more individualistic/subjective approach associated with Weber with the more collective approach of Comte, Spencer and their successors.

Michel Foucault (1926-1984). French polymath and 'poststructuralist.' Analysed the connections between language, knowledge and power in his theory of discourse, and applied these insights to the history of medicine, sexuality, psychiatry and penology (the study of prisons).

Jean-François Lyotard (1924-1998). French author of *The Postmodern Condition* (1979) which gave its name to the postmodern 'school'. Lyotard criticised the 'grand narratives' of ideology, religion, science and sociology itself and welcomed the advent of greater scepticism, relativism and 'local narratives' in the social sciences.

Judith Butler (b.1956). American social philosopher whose conceptions of 'performativity' (enacting identity) and gender as a social category (as opposed to biological sex) have had a profound effect in all branches of sociology.

'The Top Twelve' Political Thinkers in History

Plato (427-347 BC). Ancient Greek philosopher. Advocated an ideal state – based on reason and justice – and ruled by philosopher kings, in *The Republic*. Political hero: Socrates claimed that true rulers should be Philosopher Kings and believed in a strong state. His idealist views some claim influenced fascism.

Aristotle (384-322 BC). Another Ancient Greek philosopher. Author of *The Politics*, which gave equal weight to politics as it was actually practised as it did to political ideals. A student of Plato and tutor to Alexander the Great. Much more of a moderate in political terms, talked about the Goldon mean.

Augustine (354-430 AD). Roman theologian and philosopher, lived in Numidia (modern Tunisia). Viewed government as a necessary evil thanks to 'original sin', emphasised the importance of the Christian Church and personal virtue in *The City of God*.

Thomas Aquinas (1225-1274). Medieval Italian philosopher and churchman. Generally considered to have initiated many of the subsequent debates in Western philosophy about 'natural law' and 'the common good'. Very important to the Catholic Church.

Niccolò Machiavelli (1469-1527). Italian diplomat and 'Renaissance man'. Infamous for arguing that conventionally immoral 'means' were justified by the 'end' of creating a strong state. The blatantly amoral doctrine of *The Prince* was moderated, but not abandoned, in *The Discourses*, his treatise on republicanism. The true model of all modern politicians.

Thomas Hobbes (1588-1679). English philosopher. Stressed the less pleasant aspects of human nature, and advocated absolute monarchy to create social peace in *Leviathan*. With Edmund Burke (1729-1797), a forerunner of modern conservative thinking. Described life in its natural state as being 'solitary, poor, nasty, brutish and short.'

John Locke (1632-1704). Born in Somerset, Locke developed Hobbes' idea of a social contract in a more liberal direction. Advocated 'natural' rights of life, liberty and property and a separation of powers between monarch and parliament in *Two Treatises of Government*. As a philosopher, Locke was also a major influence on the school of empiricism.

Jean-Jacques Rousseau (1712-1778). Swiss philosopher who criticised modern commercial society in his *Discourse on Inequality*, and developed a sophisticated theory of popular sovereignty in *The Social Contract*. Argued that individual citizens can retain their personal freedom by submitting to a 'general will' that makes decisions in the general interest. Famously said 'Man is born free and everywhere he is in chains.'

Mary Wollstonecraft (1759-1797). English radical and supporter of the French Revolution. Argued for female emancipation in *A Vindication of the Rights of Woman* and continued the eighteenth century debate about 'manners'. Sometimes called 'the first feminist'. Said that 'mind has no sex' which is a telling phrase. Was called a 'hyena in petticoats' by a male MP.

John Stuart Mill (1806-1873). English liberal philosopher and economist. Defended free speech and individuality in *On Liberty*. Other major themes in his writings were utility (happiness), the extension of democracy and justice.

Karl Marx (1818-1883). German revolutionary; argued that the economic struggle between social classes was the dominant factor in history and was inevitably leading to a new society based on the common ownership of property (communism). Key work: *The Communist Manifesto* (1848), written with Friedrich Engels (1820-1895).

Mohandas Gandhi (1869-1948). Indian nationalist, known as 'Mahatma', meaning 'great souled'. Advocate and practitioner of passive resistance, non-violence and economic self-sufficiency based on village crafts (as opposed to modern industry). Author of *Hind Swaraj*. A significant influence on the modern anti-imperialist, peace and Green movements.

Chapter 9.
Economics.

(the study of how to use resources)

Economics has never been all that popular a subject but it had a new lease of life in the financial boom of the last twenty years. It is important because it is all really about wealth, money, production and who gets what. Think of it as being rather like how to decide what to spend money on, books or booze? Marx made economics sexy in a way but also spent much of his money on booze. He also wrote a great deal about money. Economics is often studied along with Politics and Philosophy, otherwise known as PPE. It pays to know a little bit about economics as whatever wealth you might accrue can be seriously affected by economic developments.

Some key questions.

Is economics boring?
Is it a science?
Why did they all get it so spectacularly wrong
with the global credit crunch?
Will studying economics get you a very well
paid job in the city?
How much will my student loan actually cost me
over twenty-five years?

Here are the most important economists of all time.

Adam Smith was born in 1723 and is known as the father of modern economics. He more or less invented Classical economics, the idea of the free market, the division of labor, and the "invisible hand". It is the idea that markets operate by their own laws, and rationally, that underpins all subsequent theory.

Alfred Marshal was born in 1842 and was the founder of neoclassical economics. His *Principles of Economics* (1890) was the standard textbook for a very long time. He introduced a rigorous mathematical basis to economics, defined costs of production, marginal utility and the idea of supply and demand.

John Maynard Keynes was born in 1883 and is one of the most influential economists of twentieth century. Keynesian economics is macro- economics, or in other words the ways in which the state and the economy inter-act. His contributions are *Macroeconomics, Keynesian Economics, Liquidity preference, Spending multiplier* and *Aggregate Demand-Aggregate Supply Model.*

David Ricardo was born in 1772 and was one of the most influential of the classical economists. Perhaps his most important contribution was the law of comparative advantage, a fundamental argument in favor of free trade. His Law of Diminishing Returns is the best theory for every student to know in terms of the rate of returns from production factors.

Milton Friedman was born in 1912, he was well known among scholars for his contributions - theoretical and empirical research, especially consumption analysis, monetary history and theory, and for his demonstration of the complexity of stabilization policy.

Joseph Eugene Stiglitz was born in 1943 and is an American Economist. He won the Nobel Memorial Prize in Economic Sciences in the year 2001. Critic of free markets, de-regulated globalisation and lack of public knowledge of banking. His major contributions were on screening, taxation, and unemployment.

Thomas Robert Malthus was born in 1766 in England. He contributed a lot to modern economics in the fields of demography, macroeconomics and evolutionary economics. *An Essay on the Principle of Population* sets out his main ideas on the natural limts of growth.

Joan Violet Robinson was born in 1903 and was a post-Keynesian economist. Well know for the knowledge of monetary economomics. Some of her major works were - *The Economics of Imperfect Competition* (1933), *An Essay on Marxian Economics* (1942), *Accumulation of Capital* (1956) and many more.

Karl Heinrich Marx was born in 1818. He was a German philosopher, political economist, historian, political theorist, sociologist, communist, and revolutionary. His contribution to modern economics is considerable and his works includes the ideas of surplus value, alienation and exploitation of the worker. Famous works, *The Communist Manifesto*, *Das Kapital*, and particularly the materialist conception of history.

Frederich Hayek was born in 1899. Most of Hayek's work from the 1920s through the 1930s was in the Austrian theory of Business Cycles, capital theory, and monetary theory. Hayek saw a connection between all three of these, something other economists ignored. He was interested in how people co-ordinate their activites (somewhat like Keynes).

Here is a list of the top five ranked articles by citation listed by the University of Conneticutt Department of Economics. This makes clear what interests current economists.

1. Lucas, Robert Jrunior, 1988. "On the mechanics of economic development," Journal of Monetary Economics, Elsevier, vol. 22(1), pages 3-42, July. 1785

2. Arellano, Manuel & Bond, Stephen, 1991. "Some Tests of Specification for Panel Data: Monte Carlo Evidence and an Application to Employment Equations," Review of Economic Studies, Blackwell Publishing, vol. 58(2), pages 277-97, April.1553

3. Heckman, James J, 1979. "Sample Selection Bias as a Specification Error," Econometrica, Econometric Society, vol. 47(1), pages 153-61, January. 1461

4. Mankiw, N Gregory & Romer, David & Weil, David N, 1992. "A Contribution to the Empirics of Economic Growth," The Quarterly Journal of Economics, MIT Press, vol. 107(2), pages 407-37, May.

5. N. Gregory Mankiw & David Romer & David N. Weil, 1992. "A Contribution to the Empirics of Economic Growth," NBER Working Papers 3541, National Bureau of Economic Research, Inc. 1390

6. Paul Romer, 1991. "Endogenous Technological Change," NBER Working Papers 3210, National Bureau of Economic Research, Inc.

From the Repec site of the University of Coneticutt Department of Econmoics (http://ideas.repec.org/top/).

Economics is clearly quite a technical subject but having some notion of what it is about really is essential.

One key way to approach it is to think about this question (which often occupies students) what is money and where does it come from?

Ten big ideas

1) How Markets Work
(neo-classical economics).

2) How Prices Emerge.
(what are things worth)

3) Incentives Matter.
(why people do things)

4) Comparative Advantage.
(why some things work
better than others)

5) Understanding Costs.
(what is an opportunity cost?)

6) The Division of Labour.
(who does what)

7) The Invisible Hand of the Market.
(how markets are rational)

8) What is Money? (what it does.)

9) Macro-Economics (what can the state do?)

10) Supply and Demand
(who wants things and why)

Chapter 10.
Science

Some Key ideas.

All Scientists are sceptics (or should be).
Science proceeds through observation, experimentation and analysis.
Here is the basic game plan for science:

Collect evidence (experimental data).
Create a model to explain evidence.
Use model to predict what will happen.
If the prediction doesn't work, change the model.

Science goes back to mathematics which is an abstract form of reasoning. Science has tended to grow apart from the Humanities and to see itself as 'hard' knowledge. Science is now integral to everything that happens in modern society.

Becoming an undergraduate means that you are about to become an educated citizen of the world, a fully paid up member of the universal brotherhood of knowledge. It is a fact worth repeating that you can't really know anything about the world unless you know something about science. Even if you are studying Ancient Icelandic Sagas, or golf management, you really do need to have a vague sense of the impact of science on the contemporary world. The reason for this is that science, technology and industrialization are intimately inter-connected, shaping the world we live in, as well the shape of golf clubs. Icelandic sagas influenced Tolkien who in turn influenced computer games, which in turn seem to have influenced education. Science, or the art of thinking clearly about the nature of the world, and the Universe, is a relatively recent activity in human development and can be defined as a systematic approach to modelling reality. This approach uses observation and experimentation to describe and explain natural phenomena, but seeks clear knowledge. Some people say that philosophy asks why things happen as they do and that science attempts to explain how they happen. That is another discussion however.

The Babylonians, Indians and Egyptians all contributed to early science and the Greeks, particularly Plato and Aristotle, clarified much of what was known in earlier times. Arab cultures kept science alive whilst the Europeans blew out the lights and indulged in what was known as the 'dark ages' when for some centuries Europe pretended not to know anything. After the Renaissance, and particularly because of the work of Leonardo de Vinci, Europeans decided that science was the new black and began the long process of seemingly discovering everything, from the power of steam to the basic structures of the Universe (which is supposedly strings). Despite being irritating Bill Bryson's *A Short History of Nearly Everything* is really a pretty good introduction to many things about science, particularly for the non-scientific, face-book loving generation. Everyone has heard of Einstein but hardly anybody understands the general theory of relativity, let alone special relativity, but it helps to know that Homer Simpson encountered it and got quite a good grasp. It just means that space and time are generally a bit slippier than we thought earlier, and that the Universe is larger, and more complicated, than we imagined (see *The Universe*, Richard Osborne).

So, in the interests of science, this chapter will introduce some of the key scientists and major ideas that you should really know about even for understanding everyday culture and life in the twenty-first century. Climate change is the most obvious example of the need to know something about science and the debate about whether it exists really depends on scientific knowledge versus vague opinion and mystical mumbo-jumbo. The real question is precisely what makes things tick, what causes this matter to react with that matter and produce an explosion or a tornado. (Have you noticed how climate change sceptics never suck on exhaust pipes to prove how harmless CO_2 emissions are?)

One might add that science and drugs also have a rather interesting connection, from the discovery of Cocaine in the 19th century to the creation of LSD, MDMA and all those other strange things that people ingest to alter their sense of reality. Add in computers and mobile phones and you have quite a bit of the contemporary culture covered. And at the final frontier we have the question of whether there is life on other planets and whether the Universe will really implode at some point- probably not just yet. There is also an interesting question about the contemporary representation of scientists, such as the 'mad scientist' or geek idea, as represented in *The Big Bang Theory* and *Doctor Who* show. Images of science in popular culture are not of course properly representative of what science is about. It is an important question in contemporary culture how science is perceived and understood. The nature of scientific knowledge also changes rapidly; Science is dynamic. Not everything you learned growing up is 'true' today.

The most important philosophical debates today are around the limits of science. Issues such as cloning, creating artificial life, cybernetics and what science can produce in terms of technology replicating nature. Strangely science is less and less taught in contemporary schools, which is also a question for the humanities.

Here is the world's shortest list of science's impact on the world.

Calenders probably kicked it off (planning farming).
Writing led to newspapers and popular culture.
Maps led to finding the rest of the world.
Alcohol led to getting lost again.
The Wheel led to things going round in circles.
Iron led to swords and war.
Electricity led to television.

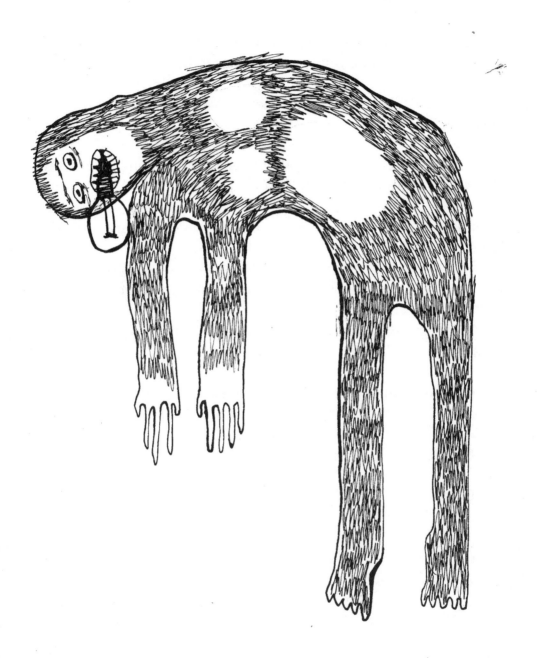

Here is very basic timeline of the major events in scientific development.

Pythagoras applies mathematics to most things
(probably the single biggest advance ever. 5th C. BC).

Aristotle talks about examining the real world of observing
(4th C. BC).

Archimedes has a 'eureka moment' which begins the science of
calculating things (3rd C. BC).

Arab philosophers applied mathematics to architecture
(7th-13th Century).

Invention of the telescope leads to cosmology and microscopes.

The Invention that kicked off the Industrial Revolution -
Steam Engines Make the World Go Around.

The Greatest Idea in Science - 17th Century – *Newton* invents
Gravity ($FG = Gm1m2/r2$) calculus and laws of motion.

The Greatest Idea in Energy - 18th Century – Electricity.

The Greatest Idea in Science - 19th Century -
Maxwell's Equations Electromagnetism.

Darwin thinks up the idea of 'natural selection' making the 19th
cent the best ever for science.

X-Rays are discovered which leads to atomic theory (19th).

The Greatest Idea in the 20th Century - Special Relativity Leads
to a Nuclear World (*Einstein*).

The Idea that began the Computer Revolution - and the Greatest Invention in the Second Half of the 20th Century – Transistors.

The Greatest Idea at the Beginning of the 21st Century - String Theory Makes the Tiniest Vibrations.

The Greatest Unknown - Science and the Beginning of Time – The Big Bang.

Here are some key ideas in science that everyone should know.

Gravity

As Newton discovered things fall downwards, and the question is why? Apparently every year several people are killed by falling coconuts, and many more by falling off ladders doing DIY. Understanding gravity would improve their life chances. What goes up must come down is a good motto in this area.

Electricity

Is a force, discovering how it worked transformed the world, and lit it up. Invisible, complex and peculiar – led to the idea of non-visible forces. Also led to all sorts of technology and ultimately understanding atomic structure.

Relativity

The rather awkward fact that whilst some things, like taxes, remain constant it seems that time and space aren't as fixed as they seem, which upsets obsessive people all over the place. Could be a good excuse for a late essay.

Motion

Why and how things move is a complex question and understanding force and energy are central to science. As an 18 year old you will probably have moved about 172,557,726,102 meters. But it is a well known fact that moving a student at 8.30 am defies most laws of motion – see relativity.

Some Key quotes from some key scientists which pretty much covers all the ground.

Definition of science:

Science is organized knowledge.
Education by Herbert Spencer (1820-1903) English philosopher.

Science is the systematic classification of experience.
George Henry Lewes (1817-78) English writer and critic.

Science is nothing but developed perception, interpreted intent, common sense rounded out and minutely articulated.
The Life of Reason by George Santayana (1863-1952) U. S. philosopher and writer.

Science is facts; just as houses are made of stone, so is science made of facts; but a pile of stones is not a house, and a collection of facts is not necessarily science.
Jules Henri Poincaré (1854-1912) French mathematician.

Science is a great game. It is inspiring and refreshing. The playing field is the universe itself.
Isidor Isaac Rabi (1898-1988) U. S. physicist. Nobel prize 1944.

Science is what you know. Philosophy is what you don't know.
Bertrand Russell (1872-1970) English philosopher, mathematician.

Science is the desire to know causes.
William Hazlitt (1778-1830) English essayist.

Science is an imaginative adventure of the mind seeking truth in a world of mystery.
Sir Cyril Herman Hinshelwood (1897-1967) English chemist. Nobel prize 1956.

Science is the knowledge of consequences, and dependence of one fact upon another.
Thomas Hobbes (1588-1679) English philosopher, author.

Quotes About Science

It is a well known fact that the universe is not only queerer than we think, but queerer than we can imagine. Why we persist in thinking the world is simple and organised is one of those questions that puzzles many scientists.

Here are some quotes about what science is actually about:

Shall I refuse my dinner because I do not fully understand the process of digestion?
Oliver Heaviside (1850-1925) English physicist.

There is no adequate defense, except stupidity, against the impact of a new idea.
Percy Williams Bridgman (1882-1961) U. S. physicist, Nobel Prize 1946.

Those who have an excessive faith in their theories or in their ideas are not only poorly disposed to make discoveries, but they also make very poor observations.
Claude Bernard (1813-78) French physiologist, 1865.

In Science the credit goes to the man who convinces the world, not to the man to whom the idea first occurred.
Sir William Osler (1849-1919) Canadian physician.

The hypotheses we accept ought to explain phenomena which we have observed. But they ought to do more than this: our hypotheses ought to foretell phenomena which have not yet been observed.
William Whewell (1794-1866) English mathematician, philosopher.

It is a popular delusion that the scientific enquirer is under an obligation not to go beyond generalisation of observed facts...but anyone who is practically acquainted with scientific work is aware that those who refuse to go beyond the facts, rarely get as far.
Thomas Henry Huxley (1825-95) English biologist.

We see only what we know.
Johann Wolfgang von Goethe (1749-1832) German poet, dramatist.

Science increases our power in proportion as it lowers our pride.
Claude Bernard (1813-78) French physiologist.

We know very little, and yet it is astonishing that we know so much, and still more astonishing that so little knowledge can give us so much power.
Bertrand Russell (1872-1970) English philosopher, mathematician.

... the scientist would maintain that knowledge in of itself is wholly good, and that there should be and are methods of dealing with misuses of knowledge by the ruffian or the bully other than by suppressing the knowledge.
Percy Williams Bridgman (1882-1961) U. S. physicist, Nobel Prize, 1946.

Physics is very muddled again at the moment; it is much too hard for me anyway, and I wish I were a movie comedian or something like that and had never heard anything about physics!
Wolfgang Pauli (1900-1958) Austrian Physicist in the US. (Nobel Prize, 1935). From a letter to R. Kronig, 25 May 1925.

I do not like it, and I am sorry I ever had anything to do with it.
Erwin Schrödinger (1887-1961) Austrian physicist. Nobel Prize, 1933. Speaking of quantum mechanics.

Those who are not shocked when they first come across quantum mechanics cannot possibly have understood it.
Niels Henrik David Bohr (1885-1962) Danish physicist.

If anybody says he can think about quantum problems without getting giddy, that only shows he has not understood the first thing about them.
Niels Henrik David Bohr (1885-1962) Danish physicist.

Penetrating so many secrets, we cease to believe in the unknowable. But there it sits nevertheless, calmly licking its chops.

H. L. Mencken (1880-1956) American journalist, writer. In: Minority Report (1956).

An ocean traveler has even more vividly the impression that the ocean is made of waves than that it is made of water.

Arthur S. Eddington (1882-1944) English astronomer and physicist.

In: The Nature of the Physical World, Cambridge (1929).

The rotating armatures of every generator and motor in this age of electricity are steadily proclaiming the truth of the relativity theory to all who have ears to hear.

Leigh Page (1884-1952) American physicist. In: American Journal of Physics, 43, 330 (1975).

I have also a paper afloat, with an electromagnetic theory of light, which, till I am convinced to the contrary, I hold to be great guns.

James Clerk Maxwell (1831-1879) Scottish physicist. In a letter to C. H. Cay, 5 January 1865.

Innocence about Science is the worst crime today.

Sir Charles Percy Snow (1905-80) English novelist and scientist.

What's the go of that? What's the particular go of that?

James Clerk Maxwell (1831-1879) Scottish physicist. Comments made as a child expressing his curiousity about mechanical things and physical phenomena.

Why are things as they are and not otherwise?

Johannes Kepler (1571-1630) German astronomer.

What is is what must be.

Gottfried Wilhelm von Leibnitz (1646-1716) German philosopher and mathematician.

We are in the ordinary position of scientists of having to be content with piecemeal improvements: we can make several things clearer, but we cannot make anything clear.

Frank Plumpton Ramsay.

*One had to be a Newton to notice that the moon is falling,
when everyone sees that it doesn't fall.*

Paul Valéry (1871-1945) French poet and philosopher.

*Nature and Nature's laws lay hid in night,
God said: "Let Newton be!", and all was light.*

Alexander Pope (1688-1744) English poet.

*To say that a man is made up of certain chemical elements is a
satisfactory description only for those who intend to use him as
a fertilizer.*

Hermann Joseph Muller (1890-1967) U. S. geneticist. Nobel prize for medicine 1946.

*When we try to pick out anything by itself, we find it is tied to
everything else in the universe.*

John Muir (1838-1914) U. S. naturalist, explorer.

*A man gazing at the stars is proverbially at the mercy of the
puddles in the road.*

Alexander Smith (1865-1922) U.S chemist.

*It is a capital mistake to theorise before one has data. Insensibly one begins to twist facts to suit theories instead of theories
to suit facts.*

Sherlock Holmes, the fictional creation of Arthur Conan Doyle (1859-1930) British physician
and novelist.

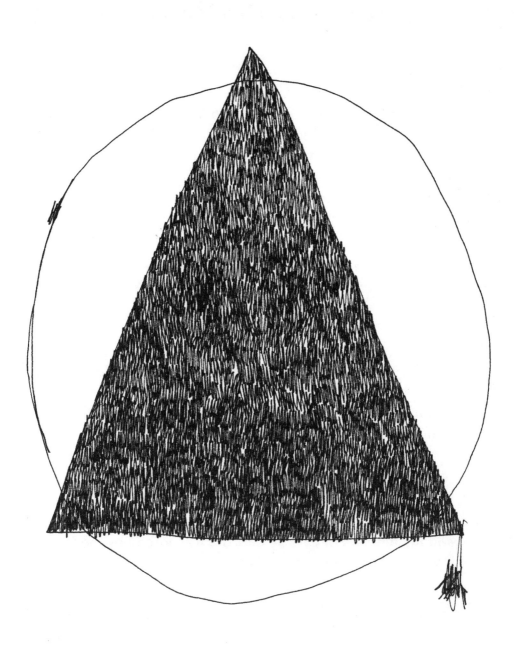

'The Top Twenty' Scientists in History

Archimedes (287-212 BC)
Greek physicist who discovered that a floating body receives a force equivalent to the weight of liquid it displaces (his 'eureka' moment!). Also famous for inventing the Archimedean screw and calculating the correct value of Pi.

Ptolemy (2nd Century BC)
Egyptian astronomer, most famous for developing a cosmology which assumed that the stars and planets (as well as the moon) orbited a fixed, spherical earth. This was the predominant view amongst scientists until the Renaissance.

Nicolaus Copernicus (1473-1543)
Polish astronomer who overturned Ptolemy's model and argued that the Earth rotated on an axis and (with the other planets) orbited the sun. This heliocentric (sun-centred) view was the foundation of modern astronomy.

Galileo Galilei (1564-1642)
Italian physicist. Made numerous experimental studies of motion. Constructed an astronomical telescope, and made observations that confirmed the theories of Copernicus, but was forced by the Catholic Church to renounce the heliocentric view.

William Harvey (1578-1657)
English anatomist and founder of modern medicine. Gave the first scientific account of the function of the human heart as a pump causing blood to circulate round the body; earlier figures had speculated this was the case, but got various details wrong.

Isaac Newton (1642–1727)

English mathematician and physicist. Discovered a verifiable theory of gravity (the story of the apple) and expounded three laws of motion. Made important contributions to optics and invented both calculus and the reflecting telescope. Often seen as one of the rationalist founders of 'the Enlightenment', but also had mystical and alchemist beliefs.

Carolus Linnaeus (1707–1778)

Swedish naturalist who invented the binomial system of classification of plants and animals; using one name for the genus, or biological type, and one name for the species. Hence, Panthera (big cat) Tigris (eastern) is the technical name for a tiger!

Antoine Lavoisier (1743–1794)

French chemist and founder of modern chemistry. Discovered oxygen and identified its role in both fire (combustion) and animal breathing (respiration). Established the distinction between the irreducible elements (e.g. gold, carbon and oxygen) and compounds (e.g. water and carbon dioxide).

Charles Babbage (1791–1871)

English mathematician and computer pioneer. The most controversial choice in this list as he received relatively little acclaim in his own time (although this also applies to Mendel). However, his mechanical calculating engines are now frequently acknowledged as important predecessors of modern computers.

Michael Faraday (1791–1867)

English chemist who first used electricity to break up the compounds Lavoisier had discovered through a process called electrolysis. He also worked on hydrocarbons, optics and electro-magnetism, and his improvements to the dynamo and discovery of benzol in 1825 helped to lay the foundation for the motoring and chemical industries.

Charles Darwin (1809-1882)

English naturalist whose theory of the natural selection of random, inherited variations overturned both religious creationism and the older theory of biological evolution based on the inheritance of environmental determined characteristics invented by the French zoologist, Jean-Baptiste Lamarck (1744-1829).

Gregor Mendel (1822-1884)

Austrian monk and botanist. Thanks to rigorous experiments with the cross-breeding of peas, laid the foundations of modern genetics by developing a theory of inheritance involving dominant and recessive traits. Like Babbage, his fame was largely posthumous.

Louis Pasteur (1822-1895)

French chemist who developed a process for destroying harmful bacteria in milk, known as pasteurisation; and invented vaccines against rabies and anthrax, building on the earlier work of Edward Jenner (1749-1823) who created a vaccine against smallpox.

Heinrich Hertz (1857-1894)

German physicist who confirmed the existence of electromagnetic waves via his experiments with coils and antennae. Hertz laid the foundations for the invention of radio by Guglielmo Marconi (1874-1937) and television by John Logie Baird (1888-1946).

Marie Curie (1867-1934) née Sklodowska

Polish (subsequently French) scientist whose pioneering studies of radioactivity made a major contribution to modern medicine; specifically leading to the establishment of radiography. Often working with her husband, Pierre, she was particularly associated with uranium, polonium and radium.

Ernest Rutherford (1871-1937)

A New Zealand born scientist, who also worked on radioactivity, and pioneered atomic fission. He identified the nuclear composition of the atom, which had generally been assumed to be the most basic particle of matter. Colloquially speaking, he 'split the atom' (a nitrogen atom) under controlled conditions in 1917.

Albert Einstein (1879-1955)

German, later American, physicist. Developed the general theory of relativity, which integrated earlier ideas on motion, time, mass and energy, while at the same time being revolutionary. The relationship between mass and energy was expressed in his famous equation $E=MC^2$. Basically re-wrote the way in which physics thought about the Universe, especially about space and time.

Alan Turing (1912-1954)

English mathematician and computer scientist. Devised the theoretical basis of modern computers ('the Universal Turing Machine') and made several important contributions to the early development of computer programming. Also involved in deciphering German code in the second WW and invented the 'Turing Test' for artifical intelleigence.

Francis Crick (1916-2004)

English biologist who discovered how genetic information is stored in molecular form as DNA (Deoxyribonucleic acid) in 1953 in collaboration with James Watson. Other researchers were working in the same field, but Crick and Watson ascertained the precise character of the double-helix structure.

James Watson (b.1924)

American biologist and collaborator of Crick's. Subsequently helped to initiate the 'Human Genome Project' based in Maryland USA in 1990; a project which seeks to map and understand the chemical pairs (genes) that determine much (some say all) of human heredity.

Chapter 11.
Globalization

World cultures and Globalization

What do you actually know about the world; and how did you acquire
that knowledge?

The process of acquiring knowledge is one of the key skills that you
should, in fact, learn at university; indeed it is the single most important
strategic skill there is. Being able to distinguish between media stories,
general ideas and real knowledge is a transferable skill that is worth its
weight in massive student debt. Those who do not learn to distinguish
dross from gold end up buying Heat magazine to try and keep warm.
Whilst at university one of the important things you have the chance to
understand is that all public knowledge is controlled and has an agenda.
This allows you the opportunity to decipher that information, and to
question the knowledge released into the public domain. No knowledge
is actually completely legitimised. By whom, where and why has this
information come into the public consciousness? University allows time
to question the authenticity of your mindset and attempt to comprehend
the opposing views of fundamentally different cultures. There is a
serious question about whether the didactic nature of the media has
become an inherent part of Western education and if so at what cost to
the global community?

University can be a social bubble in which the concerns of the outside
world seem both distant and irrelevant. To avoid this all students should
buy at least one (broadsheet) newspaper a week. Read it, question
it, and understand that white men control most of the information we
receive and that other ethnic groups and women are peripheral. This
will allow you to establish both a political understanding of your society
and a realisation of the bias by which we report news from the rest of
the world. If we do not question the knowledge that is given to us in all
forms then we cannot hope to decode the complex nature of culture,
society and what it is to be human. If by the end of your course you leave
without forming a perspective then you have missed an opportunity, your
degree becomes a collection of knowledge without purpose.

Education

Education is important to the progress of the state and the individual. Personal development comes from a greater knowledge base, providing opportunity for economic stability and satisfaction through work. The social benefits are the development of a skilled and saleable workforce creating social cohesion based on a shared ideology. Education is the key to progress and with increased levels of literacy come increased levels of opportunity. Countries that have created a coherent education system have a higher GNI (Gross National Income), higher life expectancy and low levels of undernourished peoples.

Satatistics give an overview of human education but it must be considered that the levels of testing will differ between countries as will their definitions of literate and non-literate.

	Primary Enrolment %		Secondary Enrolment %		Literacy %	
Country	Male	Female	Male	Female	Male	Female
Argentina	99	98	76	82	99	99
China	99	99	75	76	99	99
India	92	86	59	45	84	68
Indonesia	97	94	59	58	99	99
Iran	92	86	59	49	98	97
Niger	46	43	9	6	52	23
S. Africa	87	87	58	65	94	94
UK	99	99	94	97	99	99
USA	92	93	88	90	99	99

UniCEF statistics: http://www.unicef.org/infobycountry/index.html

Health

The overall health of a country's population can be measured in various ways: Life expectancy is an indicator of the general health of the adult population. Infant mortality rates depict the standard of health care in a country and indicate deprivation amongst children. The percentage of the population with clean drinking water and the percentage with improved sanitation is an expression of the country's level of need. However, to analyse the health of a country thoroughly it would be necessary to compare rates of fatal diseases such as HIV, Diarrhoea, Measles. Malnutrition in the under five's exacerbates the general health of a countries population.

Country	Life Expectancy: Age	Infant mortality rate per 1000 births	% of population improved drinking water	% of population improved sanitation	% Under 5's under-weight moderate/ severe
UK	79	5	100	100	-
Canada	81	5	100	100	-
Cuba	78	11	91	98	4
Nigeria	47	97	47	30	29
Iraq	59	36	77	76	8
Philippines	72	23	93	78	21

UniCEF statistics: http://www.unicef.org/infobycountry/index.html

Aid

Condensing Aid statistics into two paragraphs is somewhat difficult. Aid like all other areas of globalization and world cultures is dependent on relationships between countries, religious unity, governmental practices and allegiances as well as a country's level of need. The Organisation for Economic Co-operation and Development's (OECD) is made up of thirty of the most economically developed countries in the world. It is supported by the European Union (EU) and discusses the universal standards for giving aid. The Paris Declaration in 2005 created a framework for giving aid which includes allowing developing countries to use their own strategies to stimulate growth and independence. This also means that donor countries have to align themselves to the developing countries objectives creating duel responsibility. Critics of this process say that Non-Governmental Organisations (NGO's) should control the transportation and organisation of aid into developing countries. They believe, that this will dissuade corruption and allow agencies without a political alignment to dispatch money into the right areas. However, without the responsibility of aid managed by the governments of developing countries politicians have no responsibility to those in poverty within their countries. A duel programme of care allows the donor country to expect results and evidence whilst the developing country has ultimate control of aid distribution. Without an aid system that relies on the richest countries in the world giving to the poorest there would be catastrophic effects. With increased poverty comes increased domestic competition which can lead to discrimination and ultimately conflict. The obvious effects of malnutrition increase contraction of HIV, measles, diarrhoea causing greater infant mortality rates and decreased life expectancy. Without Aid there is an increased need for asylum which puts pressure on developed countries and can promote political extremism.

Trade

International trading has become crucial in sustaining a westernised lifestyle ensuring we can all eat strawberries in the middle of winter or pomegranates all year round. Unfortunately, this comes at a cost to developing countries who farm products that we demand instead of producing crops to feed their own people. This process of 'cash for crops' encourages farmers to grow more expensive products such as tobacco and cotton rather than practical solutions to famine like cereals and vegetables. World trade statistic show that developing countries who export over 80% of their agricultural and manufactured production, also import a high percentage of their required consumables. This demonstrates the need for a reassessment of the commodities traded. If these countries decreased their exports and focused on a more intrinsic farming culture they could create practical solutions to domestic problems and a higher level of self sufficiency. However, the country's GNI would decrease, discouraging international trade and isolating them from the international market. Once isolated, their global position is compromised and their access to aid can be restricted. The ethics of international trade are therefore complex; finding a fine balance between producing enough food whilst staying part of the worldwide community is a continuing battle.

The five most highly traded items are: oil (petroleum products), coffee, steel and infrastructure, gold and wheat. To quantify the amount of oil traded, the USA consumed 20,680,000 barrels of oil per day in 2007. Imported: 13,710,000 barrels per day, exported: 1,165,000 barrels per day.

Religion

Religion influences all other areas of world cultures and globalization. The alliance of countries sharing a predominant belief system has become apparent through the giving of aid, support in times of conflict and increased trading. It is also an influence on education restricting the release of knowledge in line with a belief system. This has created religious communities with power more than individual nation states and influence over a great number of people. The growth of multiculturalism may have encouraged the realignment with religion as a feature of identity. Contemporary society has evolved over the last 30 years to include a diverse collection of multicultural people who can no longer define themselves according to a common ethnicity, which could leave a cultural void. This has led to a newly emerging dependence on religion. Complete alignment to a particular religious denomination can cause domestic and international conflict between opposing religions. The continuing troubles between Catholics and Protestants or Sunni and Shi'a Muslim's demonstrate the power of a fundamental emergence into religious law.

Country	Number of devotee's to Religion
Christianity	2 179 million
Islam	1 292 million
Hinduism	957 million
Buddhism	396 million
Sikhism	23 million
Judaism	13 million
Other	825 million
Non-Religious	1 018 million

Religion statistics www.adherant.com

Environment

The state of the world's environment has become a prominant debate over the last ten years, becoming a point of contention for political parties. Figures suggest that if there is not a dramatic decrease in carbon emissions by 2050 then the Earth's temperature will rise by 2°C causing the polar ice caps to melt. This will result in a series of natural disasters echoing the Asian Tsunami and the flooding in New Orleans. To avoid this, experts say that we must reduce our emissions by at least 80% across the entire globe. However, the reduction of a countries CO_2 can only happen with the increase of renewable energy sources; wind, waves and sun. Critics are concerned renewable energy sources are ill-equipped to deal with the high demand for energy.

This debate has led to developed countries whose carbon emissions are high to off-set their pollution onto developing countries. The UN's Intergovernmental Panel on Climate Change credits countries whose emissions are below the required rate and indebts countries such as the US and the UK whose emissions are over six times the approved rate per capita. Environmentalists fear that the results of global warming will affect countries prone to drought (Northern Africa and the Middle East) or those closest to sea level (Bangladesh, Vietnam) but that it is these countries that have a low Carbon debt. Droughts and floods will create unsolvable problems such as the need for food and clean drinking water for an ever increasing world population.

Conflict

Conflict is a tool of politics that should be used after the breakdown of all other political processes. This means that conflicts arising between differing ideologies or between religions should proceed through all other forms of global diplomacy before war is declared. Although the world is more peaceful now that at any time since World War I, ongoing conflicts follow the same pattern of diplomatic breakdown, causing armed warfare. This displaces great numbers of civilians and promotes fundamentalist thinking. Most of the wars being fought across the world are intrastate or civil wars. These tend to be caused by race or religious animosities causing ideological differences. Africa has been particularly affected by civil wars. Conflict has made agricultural production problematic due to lack of farming possibilities in conflict areas. The danger caused by going out has prohibited children from gaining an education. Difficulties getting into countries have restricted aid and the chance to trade with the global community. Warfare affects all areas of globalisation and world culture cutting off individual states or countries from the international community. Unlike during WWI when the percentage of civilians killed was 5% in modern warfare 75% of those injured are non-combatant or women and children. These figures suggest that arms have become more sophisticated at killing large numbers of people with little effort, resulting in the accurate destruction of a country and its people.

Chapter 12.
Art

Studying art at University, or at an art college, has changed dramatically over the last thirty years from being a quite extreme minority activity to a very popular option which includes all the new digital media options and designer possibilities. Art History has almost disappeared and most art colleges have become the sort of universities where instead of studying painting or drawing students do things like Personal and Professional development or Excell spreadsheets and CV writing. Graphic Design, Multi-Media Communication and the Design Information revolution have changed the laid back face of art colleges into swishy, aluminium, designer interface research inter-active knowledge transfer hubs. The old idea of hanging about waiting for inspiration is long gone. Futurising is what goes on in the arts today; there are so many art students that there are enough people to staff four hundred Renaissances every three years. If you are going to do the Arts at University try and be realistic about the job prospects afterwards; how many Graphic designers does the world actually need? Look at the real job prospects in your choosen field and get past the Saatchi dream that, come the Degree show, you will be discovered and become rich. In itself, Art is an interesting field but extra strategic thinking is needed in choosing courses and being certain of the direction you choose.

Art itself is an area that all students should know something about, from Greek statues to Anthony Gormley's metal people art is about representations of how we define the human condition. Art can be seen as a sort of visual shorthand for all aspects of human culture. From religion to sexuality and utopian dreams art seeks to turn ways of seeing into ways of thinking visually.

Art History

From scratches on cave walls, which probably represented ideas about hunting, people have always sought to create pictures of the world and to make sense of it. Art is the visual history of the world and of the ways in which people have conceptualised what we think and see. So art history is about deciphering the kinds of art that people have made and of thinking about why they did it in that particular way. You can just appreciate art for what it is or you need to start thinking where it all came from and why. The literal history of art is lost in the mists of time; just recently some Australian aboriginal artworks have been discovered that appear to be the oldest in the world.

"A red ochre depiction of two giant extinct birds on an overhanging rock in northern Australia could be one of the oldest paintings in the world. Scientists have calculated the artwork, slightly smudged after thousands of years in the wilderness, pre-dates European settlement in Australia and could be up to 40,000 years old." *The Times*, June 1st 2010.

For rather interesting historical reasons many people feel intimidated by art, they feel mystified by its complexities, but that is simply because of unfamiliarity. One way to approach art is to just look at it and think about what impact it has on you; later you can learn the history. It's a bit like Opera, you can listen to the great tunes and love it without knowing anything about it. Afterwards you can dig as deep as you like into the history and the technical side of it.

In essence we could say that art is a bit like cooking, you take different elements, mix them together and try and produce perfect dishes. A similar activity happens when the elements of art are sensibly combined. Instead of complex spices and meats you've basically got line, shape, form, space, texture, value and colour. Artists manipulate these elements, mix them in with principles of design and compose a piece of art. Not every work has all of these elements in it, but there are always at least two present. Art, in other words, is about designing and representing ideas and emotions in a visual language, rather than a spoken one.

Summary of Art History.

Ancient man makes patterns on bones and walls.
Religious objects represent gods and myths. (fertility symbols)
Egyptians develop hieroglyphs and decorate tombs.
Chinese develop 'eastern' perspectives on artistic representation.
Greeks invent a new naturalistic form of art.
Byzantine Empire develops Greco-Roman art.
Arab/Muslim art develops 'sacred geometry'.
Western Christianity develops religious art.
The Renaissance returns to Greco-Roman ideas.
During the Enlightenment 'Art' is invented.
The industrial age produces 'bourgeois art'
Photography transforms the idea of art.
Twentieth century blows the idea of 'art' apart.
The moving image makes art into multi-media.
The Digital age re-writes art.

Here are the main questions that art theory and art history try to answer.

1) What does that image 'mean'?
2) Who made it, and why?
3) What is art for?
4) What is good art?
5) Why is this art superior to that art?
6) How do you historically understand a particular work of art?
7) How do you relate modern art to past art?
8) Is everything today 'art'?
9) What is the relationship between 'Eastern' and 'Western' art?
10) Why were artists mainly seen as men, and Western?
11) Why is some art worth lots of money?

Other important things about art

1. Art is as distinctively human as language and religion.

2. Man has a profound need for art, in order to imagine perfection.

3. The unique function of art is to present, in concrete form, what is essentially an abstraction. Turning emotions and ideas into art objects makes solid the possibility of imagination.

4. The point of art is, as the Objectivist Center says on it's website, that "..... a work of art can touch the deepest places in us, feelings we often have trouble defining and making explicit."

5. The many different forms of art do this by re-creating reality, and by selectively representing aspects of reality. The artist does the selecting, stylizing the scene or the image and presenting it in a certain way, with some things emphasized and others taken away. Art is the selection of one possibility from many.

6. Part of what makes art "great" is the skill of artists capturing their world view and presenting the essential concerns in their art.

7. In addition to the artist's skill, art can be judged by the ways in which it captures a 'world-view' of 'way of seeing'. Universality is one of the great aspects of art.

8. Art is an extension of man's ability to recreate the world, and himself, in a different domain, it is a form of utopian dreaming.

... World's Top 10 Greatest Painters & Sculptors. Brief notes on why and what to see ...

Michelangelo Buonarroti (1475-1564)

Clearly the greatest painter, draughtsman and sculptor of all time, Michelangelo was (along with Leonardo Da Vinci and Raphael) a key figure of the Italian High Renaissance in both Florence and Rome. His Old Testament Sistine Chapel frescoes justifiably rank as the finest body of figurative art in the history of painting. Some of his marble carvings have a flawless beauty and polish, proving his absolute technical mastery. In the field of the heroic male figure he remained for centuries (and arguably still is) the supreme exponent. Regarded with awe by most of his contemporaries, who applied the Italian word "terribilita" (frightening power) to his works, Michelangelo devoted most of his last 20 years to architecture (notably the design of St Peter's Basilica in Rome), in which his reputation is as formidable as in painting and sculpture. This extraordinary domination of the three major visual arts -a feat unlikely to be repeated- is what makes him the world's greatest ever artist.

Masterpieces of Painting/Sculpture
- Genesis (1508-12) and Last Judgement (1535-41) Sistine Chapel frescoes
- Pieta (1497-9) Marble,
Saint Peters Basilica, Rome
- David (1501-4) Marble, Galleria dell'Accademia,Florence

Rembrandt van Rijn (1606-69)

Definitely the greatest painter since the Renaissance, the Dutch Realist genius Rembrandt created a large number of powerful masterpieces, including some of the finest examples of history-painting, group and individual portraiture, genre-paintings, still-life and self-portraits ever produced in the history of art. He was one of the greatest exponents of chiaroscuro, the use of light and shadow. he is also famous for introducing a revolutionary realism into painting.

Painting Masterpieces by Rembrandt
- Jacob Blessing the Children of Joseph (1656) oil, Gemaldegallerie, Kassel
- The Nightwatch (1642) oil on canvas, Rijksmuseum, Amsterdam
- Syndics of the Cloth-Makers Guild (1662) oil, Rijksmuseum
- Self-Portrait (1669) oil on canvas, National Gallery, London

Peter Paul Rubens (1577-1640)

Described as "the prince of painters and the painter of princes."

Painting Masterpieces by Rubens
- Samson and Deliah (1609) oil on wood, National Gallery, London
- Descent from the Cross (1611-14) oil/wood, Catherdal of Our Lady, Antwerp
- Rape of the Daughters of Eluccipus (1618) oil, Alte Pinacothek, Munich.

Donatello (1386-1466)

The greatest European sculptor of the 15th century and probably the best artist of his era, Donatello was part of the remarkable group of artists (Alberti, Brunelleschi, Masaccio) who drove the early Renaissance in Florence.

Sculpture Masterpieces by Donatello
- David (c.1440) Bronze, Museo Nazionale del Bargello, Florence
- Mary Magadalene (c.1455) Painted wood, Museo Nazionale del Bargello
- Equestrian Statue of the Gattamelata (1444-53) Bronze, Piazza del Santo.

JMW Turner (1775-1851)

Almost certainly the greatest landscape painter in the history of art, he exhibited at the London Royal Academy at only 15 years of age. His innovative technical and stylistic working methods in both oils and watercolours gave his paintings a revolutionary impact, in composition, tone and form. He had a lifelong interest in the portrayal of light, and endless respect for the Old Masters. Revered by his contemporaries, including John Constable.

Painting Masterpieces by JMW Turner
- Burning of the House of Lords and Commons (1835) oil, Philadelphia Museum
- The Fighting Temeraire (1839) oil on canvas, National Gallery, London
- Snow Storm: Steamboat off a Harbour's Mouth (1842) oil, Tate Gallery

Jan Van Eyck (1390-1441)

The most acclaimed painter of the Early Netherlands School, he worked with his brother Hubert Van Eyck on the Ghent Altarpiece. He was noted especially for his pioneering mastery of oil painting, his introduction of a new realism in religious works and portraiture, and his use of luminous glowing colours. He was the supreme model of painterly technique during the early Northern Renaissance.

Painting Masterpieces by Jan Van Eyck
- Ghent Alterpiece (1432) oil on wood, Saint Bavo Catherdal, Ghent
- Man in a Red Turban (1433) oil on wood, National Gallery, London
- Portrait of Giovanni Arnolfini and His Wife (1434) oil on wood, National Gallery.

Leonardo Da Vinci (1452-1519)

He was the "Universal Renaissance Man" - Leonardo completed a mere handful of works but remained a major figure in the High Renaissance era. His oil painting technique was enormously innovative and influential, notably his supreme skill in sfumato (whereby he mellowed the precise outlines employed by previous painters), which was described by Giorgio Vasari as one of the distinguishing marks of modern painting. He was a Florentine artist, draughtsman, scientist, theorist and invented the modern role of great artist.

Painting Masterpieces by Leonardo Da Vinci
- Lady with Ermine (c.1490) oil on wood, Czartoryski Museum, Cracow
- The Last Supper (1495-98) fresco, Convent of Santa Maria delle Grazie
- Mona Lisa (1503) oil on wood, Louvre, Paris.

Claude Monet (1840-1926)

The leader and devoted adherent of the French Impressionism plein-air painting movement, and the acknowledged initiator of "Modern Art", Monet had a lifelong obsession with the depiction of light. His "Haystacks" and "Water Lily" series of canvases (the latter completed in his garden at Giverny) took years to complete. A close colleague of the Impressionist painters Pissarro and Renoir, his later works (not unlike those of Turner, whom he admired) spilled into Expressionism. Followers included Alfred Sisley, as well as Edgar Degas, Berthe Morisot, James Abbott McNeill Whistler, Georges Seurat and Edouard Vuillard.

Painting Masterpieces by Claude Monet
- Impression, Sunrise (1873) oil on canvas, Musee Marmottan Monet, Paris
- Poppies Near Argenteuil (1873) oil on canvas, Musee d'Orsay
- Haystack in the Morning, Snow Effect (1891) Museum of Fine Arts, Boston
- Waterlilly Pond (1899) oil on canvas, National Gallery, London

Auguste Rodin (1840-1917)

Whilst undoubtedly the grandafather of mod-ern scuplture Rodin began in a very traditional manner, his craft skills were sublime and his creativity enormous. Needless to say he was ignored to begin with.

Sculpture Masterpieces by Auguste Rodin
- The Thinker (1881)
Bronze, Musee Rodin, Paris
- The Kiss (1888-9)
Marble, Musee Rodin, Paris
- The Burghers of Calais (1889)
Bronze, Musee Rodin, Paris
- The Gates of Hell (1880-1917)
Musee d'Orsay, Paris

Pablo Picasso (1881-1973)

Arguably the most influential artist of the 20th century: not least because he was the most important semi-abstract artist and one of the great expressionist painters – co-founder of cubism. Picasso was a great sculptor, ceramicist, designer and printmaker, whose prolific output drew inspiration from prehistoric, tribal, classical, Renaissance and avant-garde themes. Picasso's revolutionary treatment of the picture plane (in his Cubist work) effectively started a new era of fine art, while his innovative sculptures were among the first to utilize "found" materials. These innovations had a profound effect on the development of modern and contemporary art movement including Constructivism, Futurism, Orphism, Purism and Vorticism, as well as Dada and Surrealism, and on contemporary painters (eg. Marcel Duchamp, Juan Gris, Fernand Leger, Francis Picabia, Robert Delaunay) and sculptors (eg. Archipenko, Jacques Lipchitz, and Ossip Zadkine).

Painting Masterpieces by Picasso
- Blue Nude (c.1904) oil, Picasso Museum, Barcelona
- Garcon a la Pipe (1905) oil on canvas, Private Collection
- Les Demoiselles d'Avignon (1907), oil on canvas, Museum of Modern Art NY
- Guernica (1937) oil on canvas, Prado Museum, Madrid

Chapter 13.
Top Ten

If you don't read all of the other stuff in this book here's an even more condensed version of how to get educated, by sampling the best of everything, (but you'll still have to read books, make notes, and concentrate at some point).

Obviously the ten best of everything is, at one level, really silly; because why should it be ten rather than eleven or one hundred?

That is a question about knowledge and culture which just shows that whichever way you approach it any decision you make actually implies some cultural analysis- this one is better than that one.

So, in the spirit of theoretical idiocy, trivial pursuits, and just plain learning, here's the lists of things that you should have read, viewed, or listened to.

Top Ten Books to Read.*

The Bible.
The Koran.
Don Quixote.
Crime and Punishment.
The wealth of Nations.
The Origin of the Species.
Introductory Lectures on Psychoanalysis.
Vindication of the Rights of Women.
The Rights of Man.
The Odyssey.

Top Ten Films.

The Leopard.
Apocalyspe Now.
Les Enfant du Paradis.
Rasomon.
Yol.
Andrei Rublev.
The Seventh Seal.
Citizen Kane.
Battle of Algeirs.
Modern Times.

Top Ten Theories to know.

Theory of Relativity.
Feminism.
Marxism.
Climate change.
String theory.
General theory of money.
Newton's laws.
Sod's Law.
Evolution.
Nuclear Theory.

*This means the books that are the most influential texts that have ever been written, which means both religion and knowledge

Top Ten food tips.

Rubbish in -rubbish out
is one of the laws of the Universe.
Do not eat junk food -
except in drunken emergencies.
Fresh vegetables are very cheap
and highly nutritious.
Not being able to cook proper food is sad.
Try ethnic, buy local and eat radishes-
good for the liver.
Try forming a food co-op and buying in bulk.
Raw carrots (£3 for a sack) are roughly 300%
healthier than kebabs.
Fish really is good for the brain.
Tea, especially green/black, is also healthy.
Takeaway food is expensive, processed and
injurious to the planet.

Alternative (Mainstream) Films Top Ten.

One Flew Over the Cuckoos Nest
Battleship Potemkin
2001 A Space Odyssey
Vertigo
Godfather I&II
Metropolis
The Gospel According to St. Matthew
Gone with the Wind
Birth of a Nation
Citizen Kane

Top Ten safety Tips.

Lock things up
(student homes regularly get burgled).
Don't walk home alone at night (drunk or sober).
Learn about your new locality, buses, taxis,
safe places, unsafe places.
Keep your mobile safe and charged (and hidden).
You must have insurance for electronic
stuff and travel.
Mark your stuff with numbers
(house/dob etc).
Halls of residence are targeted
don't let random people in.
Be careful at cash points
(try not to use at night).
Watch your drinks in nightclubs / pubs.
Be careful of dodgy unlicensed mini-cabs.

Plays Top Ten.

Hamlet
Three Sisters
Metamorphosis
Mother Courage
Dr Faustus
Waiting for Godot
A Doll's House
Shopping and Fucking
Top Girls
Abigale's Party

Chapter 14.
Music

This section may seem like a sweeping generalisation since it has been given the title 'music' and only concerns composers from the classical genre. The reason that we have provided you with a selection of composers is that many of them relate to other artistic, philosophical and scientific developments occurring at the time they were around. The historical significance of these people on musical development, especially in terms of western music, is undeniable. Their social significance is a piece of cultural capital that will contextualise your knowledge, giving you a rounder understanding of cultural and social development, especially in Europe. By providing you with some essential thinkers and developers in the musical field you will hopefully be able to incorporate their significance in line with the more central themes of your course. If you are doing science then you may not see the significance of this section but Arnold Schoenberg for example, was exiled from Germany along with Einstein and was accused of incorporating Einstein's theories into his compositions. These men have transcend music to become part of our social fabric and cultural makeup.

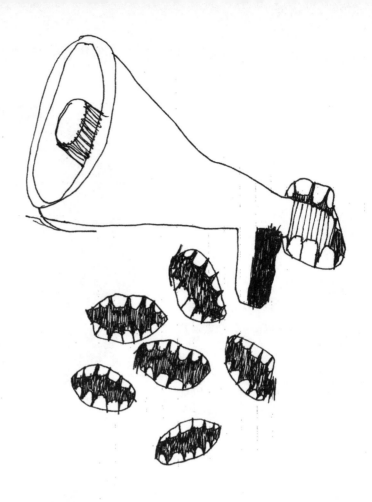

Periods in Classical Music

Renaissance – 1400 to 1600
Baroque – 1600 to 1760
Classical – 1730 to 1820
Romantic – 1815 to 1910
20th Century – 1900 to 2000
21st Century – 2000 to present

Wolfgang Amadeus Mozart

Austrian

1756–1791

Listen To
Eine Kleine Nachtmusik
Piano Concerto No.21 in C
Symphony No.40
Requiem Mass
Magic Flute (Opera)
The Marriage of Figaro
(Opera)

A child prodigy Mozart was composing works from the age of five. A court musician to various people he never settled and travelled Europe, composing constantly. One of the most influential musicians in history his presence is felt throughout the modern musical world. Mozart's music is the archetypal example of the classical style, incorporating the intricacies of baroque composing into a more rigid structure and focused aesthetic. His gregarious personality and precocious talent combined to create a persona which has become immortalised along with his fantastic music. One of his major abilities was his ability to absorb components from other composers and adapt them to his own devices. This trait was employed on his various European excursions and helped to create works with a unique musical voice. One of the essential elements of his work is the presentation of dramatic action articulated through music.

Classical Era Composer

Ludwig Van Beethoven

German

1770-
1827

Listen To
5th Symphony
9th Symphony
(Ode to Joy)
Fur Elise
Moonlight Sonata
Minuet in G

Beethoven was pivotal in the transition from 18th Century Classicism to 19th Century Romanticism. Although rooted in the traditions of Mozart and Haydn, whom he studied under, his music was a progression from these composers; attempting to encompass the literature, philosophy and ideas of the 19th Century. Throughout his life he struggled against deafness and his changeable personality, although his immense musical talent carried him through his personal troubles. Beethoven's hearing started to deteriorate in his late 20s, by the time he was 34 he was nearly completely deaf. This did not stop him from composing and some of his best received and loved works were written when he could not hear the music. Beethoven introduced the idea of illustrative music and is considered an innovator who widened the scope of music at the time. He revealed more vividly than any of his predecessors the power of music to convey a philosophy of life.

Classical Era Composer

George Friederich Handel

German

1685–
1759

Listen To
Solomon
(Arrival of the Queen
of Sheba)
Messiah
Water Music
(Suite No.2 in D minor)

Showed vast musical promise as a child and was therefore granted the opportunity to study music from an early age. Travelled extensively in Italy from 1706-10 and whilst there met and studied many of Italy's finest musicians of the day. The years in Italy greatly influenced and changed Handel's musical style, influencing his operatic compositions and gained him international acclaim. Handel moved to England in 1710 and had so much success that he decided to stay their permanently, eventually being granted an annual allowance by Queen Anne. Heavily influenced by the Italian baroque era his music has been an inspiration to many subsequent composers.

Late Baroque Era

(Franz) Joseph Haydn

Austrian

1732–
1809

Listen To
Minuet of the Ox
The Raiserquartet
The Kaiserquartet
The Creation
The Seasonsin G

One of the most important and influential composers of his time, he was vital in the development of the symphony, string quartet, piano trio and sonata and his innovations granted him the name 'father of the symphony'. Haydn lived in Austria all his life, mainly working for one family, the Esterhazy, as court composer. This lifestyle isolated him from trends and other composers which meant he had to develop his own stylistic and rhythmic nuances. Friend of Mozart and teacher of Beethoven, Haydn's lively personality and sense of humour was evident in his musical styling. Although a resident of Austria he travelled extensively around the rest of Europe. His music was bold, distinctive and changeable inspired by emotional elements and the life of the common man. He is considered one of the most prolific and important composers of all time.

Classical Era Composer

Peter Ilyitch Tchaikovsky

Russian

1840–1893

Listen To
1812 Overture
Marche Slave
Nutcracker (Ballet)
Swan Lake (Ballet)
The Sleeping Beauty (Ballet)
Eugene Onegin (Opera)

Hailing from a Middle Class Russian family he chose a musical career instead of the civil service, disappointing his family but going on to write some of the greatest and most popular works in the cannon of classical music. He wrote across a wide range of genres and although he was heavily criticised during the first half of the 20th Century his place as one of the most significant composers of all time has now been secured. Tchaikovsky had a mixed private life which saw him experience bouts of depression, this may have been due to his suppressed homosexuality, and although his death is attributed to cholera it is now believed that he committed suicide. He was the first professional Russian composer and the first Russian to think about his country's place amongst European musical culture.

Romantic Era Composer

Frederic Francois Chopin

Polish

1810–
1849

Listen To
Polonaise in A
Minute Waltz
Piano Sonata No.2 in B
Flat Minor (Funeral
March)

A piano prodigy Chopin left Poland at the age of twenty and never went back. His health was frail for the majority of his life; he died at the tender age of thirty nine. Chopin made a comfortable living as a composer and piano teacher, whilst travelling across Europe. When in Paris he had a volatile relationship with the French Author George Sand and it was Sand who introduced him to many literary, artistic and musical figures of the day. Citing Mozart and Bach as his most important musical influences the majority of his compositions are for the piano and consist of technically demanding music which is considered to epitomise the romantic style. His reputation rests on his small scale works which, in other hands, would have been mere musical trifles of the period.

Romantic Era Composer

Johann Sebastian Bach

German

1685–
1750

Listen To
Air on a G String
Brandenburg Concerto
No.3 Cello Suite No.1
Minuet in G
Cantata No.147
(Jesu, Joy of Man's Desiring)

Born into a family of prominent musicians Bach was instructed in a plethora of instruments, especially harpsichord, organ and violin, from an early age. Although he is not credited with introducing any new musical forms he brought the baroque period to a conceptual climax by adapting the German style to incorporate rhythms, forms and structures from across Europe; especially from Italy and France. Known during his lifetime throughout Europe as an organist, he was not widely celebrated as a composer until the 19th Century when a revival of his music came about, sealing his place as the major composer of the Baroque era. Revered for his intellectual depth, technical command and the artistic beauty of his work Mozart, Beethoven and Chopin were amongst his most prominent admirers. Bach was and continues to be an influence on composers and contemporary music.

.

Baroque Era Composer

John Milton Cage

American

1912–
1992

*Listen To
Polonaise in A
Minute Waltz
Piano Sonata No.2 in B
Flat Minor
(Funeral March)*

Cage was a musical pioneer and also a leading figure of the American avant-garde. He was one of the first musicians to use electronic instruments and non-standard playing techniques to enhance his music. Revolutionary in his concept of chance music; this is music where elements of the performance are left to the performers on the night. This heavily influenced by non western philosophies, especially the classic Chinese text the *I Ching*. Cage saw music as:
'Not an attempt to bring order out of chaos nor to suggest improvement in creation, but simply a way of waking up to the very life we're living.'
A conceptual artist he composed pieces for a 'prepared piano' which consisted of a normal grand piano with different objects inserted between the strings for specific effect. He had a huge cultural and aesthetic impact with his mantra that 'everything we do is music'.

20th Century Composer

Igor Fyodorovich Stravinsky

Russian

1882–
1971

Listen To
Petrushka (Ballet)
*The Rites of Spring
(Ballet)*
Orpheus
Symphony in C
The Flood

An important and influential composers of the 20th Century Stravinsky came to fame initially by composing ballets but his career is most notable for the stylistic diversity of his work. The first performance of *The Rites of Spring*, in 1913, caused riots due to its rhythmic score and scenes of Russian pagan life, made up of violent dance steps displaying primitive fertility rites. He transformed musical structure which created for him a reputation as a musical revolutionary, changing musical design. In the 1920s he turned to neoclassicism. This work took traditional forms and concealed them within new structures focusing on rhythmic energy, melody from tight notation and clarity of form. A man who had inexhaustible thirst for knowledge which has made him a vital influence on Western music from the time of his compositions to the present day.

20th Century Composer

Franz Peter Schubert

Austrian

1797–
1828

Listen To
The 5th Symphony
The 8th Symphony
(The Unfinished)
Der Erlkonig
Heiden Roslein

Schubert hailed from a musical family and received formal training from an early age. Vastly underappreciated during his life time his melody and harmonic music enjoyed a revival in the decades after his death, in the latter half of the 19th Century. As a result he has come to be considered one of the greatest western composers of all time. He died at the tender age of thirty one and was buried next to his idol Beethoven. He produced a large body of work for such a short career; although he never managed to self sustain as a musician. A creator of delightful tunes his technical ability and experimental nature only became appreciated after his death. He was always a precocious talent, when he was eighteen he composed a hundred and fifty songs in one year. Although he died in obscurity he shall be remembered and revered for his work and unquestionable influence on subsequent composers.

Romantic Era Composer

Wilhelm Richard Wagner

German

1813–
1883

Listen To
The Ring Cycle
The Rheingold
The Valkyrie
Siegfried
The Twilight of the Gods
Tristan and Isolde
Tannhauser

Wagner did not come from a musical background but was influenced by his actor step-father and as a result was drawn to the fusion of drama and music in opera. After honing his abilities he was made court composer in Dresden but as a result of the failed German revolution Wagner, who played a minor role in leftist politics, was exiled. He pioneered the concept of *Gesamtkunstwerk* or total artwork. This theory is the synthesis of all art forms, for Wagner all forms came together to serve a common purpose. He laid out these theories in his book *Opera and Drama*. This concept changed the operatic genre and is most clearly presented in his four opera collection *The Ring of Nibelung*, which Wagner wanted performed as a series. He was so focused on his vision for these operas that he built his own venue in which to stage them, the Bayreath Festival Theatre.

Romantic Era Composer

George Gershwin

1898–
1937

Listen To
Porgy and Bess
I Got Rhythm
Someone to Watch
Over Me
Rhapsody in Blue
An American in Paris

A composer who spanned the classical genre and the world of popular music by composing for both concert halls and Broadway shows. From Russian immigrant parents he was born Jacob Gershowitz. He quit school at fifteen and worked on Tin Pan Alley, home of the New York music industry, publishing music from the age of seventeen. Always seeking to work with a variety of people on experimental music he composed classical works of operatic and symphonic styles. Taking elements of European classicism and black American musical genres Gershwin transformed modern composition. His ability to adapt forms of music to his unique devices stood him apart from his contemporaries and his influence is felt throughout modern music in the amalgamation of west musical traditions and rhythm and tonality from black musicians.

20th Century Composer

Arnold Schoenberg

Austrian/American
1874– 1951

Listen To
String Quartet #2, op.10
Verklarte Nacht, op.4
Moses und Aron (Opera)
Pelleas und Melisande
(Symphonic Poem)

Schoenberg showed compositional urges from a very early age, almost immediately after starting to learn the violin at nine years old. Throughout his career he was experimental and bold in his musical expressions. He grew up and developed his talents in Berlin but with the rise of Hitler and Nazi rule his music became seen as a degenerate art form and he was forced to move to America, becoming a citizen there in 1941. His compositional style took the form of three periods, initially he was influenced by romanticism, he then undertook pioneering work into the area of atonality, music where there is no key or central tone. Finally Schoenberg developed a '12 tone' form of composition which did not focus on one central theme but on twelve notes relating only to each other. This means of ordering his work allowed his music to become simpler and clearer and as a result he is amongst the most important composers in 20th Century musical thought.

20th Century Composer

Giuseppe Fortunino Francesco Verdi

Italien

1813–
1901

Listen To
Il Travatore
Rigoletto
Requiem Mass
Nabubucco
I Lombardi

Mainly composing in operatic form his first major influences were German operas but he was a studious pupil of his craft and by incorporating French and Italian methods he developed a very European musical style. His music was not just beautiful but was politically and socially motivated, commenting on, amongst other things, Italian occupation by Austria and the balance of passion and social order. Verdi's works are most praised for their emotional intensity, melodic nature and dramatic characterisation. He transformed the face of Italian opera into a unified musical and dramatic force, making his operatic works amongst the most frequently performed in the world today. The majority of his works are the confrontation, by the protagonist, of good and evil relying on Verdi's masterful musicality and character development. A wonderful composer and definer of new operatic styles.

Romantic Era Composer

Henry Purcell

English

1659–1695

Listen To
Dido and Aeneas
(Semi-opera)
King Arthur (Semi-opera)
Te Deum
Love's Goddess
Sure Was Blind

Both Purcell's father and two of his brothers were musicians and consequently he was given first class musical training. Revelling in the period after the restoration of the monarchy in England he was employed as a court composer by the Chapel Royal, the Kings own church. A master of compositional techniques he incorporated Italian and French styles into his own work but still managed to have a definitively English musical voice. He worked in Westminster for twenty five years in the service of three kings. His style is an amalgamation of all the styles in vogue in his lifetime. His ability to craft music for words has been matched by few composers since and as a result his impression on the western musical cannon is unquestionable, even on modern musicians in the pop and rock arena.

Baroque Era Composer

Richard Osborne
is the author of many internationally
best-selling books.

Philosophy for Beginners.
Sociology for Beginners
Megawords
The Universe
Art Theory for Beginners
Philosophy in Art
Freud for Beginners
Radical Philosophy Reader
Up the British
Eastern Philosophy for Beginners.

Mary Reid
has a B.A. in Comparative Literature and Drama
from the University of Canterbury. (2008)
She is currently starting a PGCE at Sussex University
after spending two years working as a teaching
assistant.

John Reid
has an MA in English and American Literature
from the University of Canterbury. He is currently
working as a free-lance journalist and as a
teaching assitant.

Good luck at University.

Remember that studying
is both a struggle
and a reward.

Contact
stuffuniversity.com
for more information.

Other books from Zidane Press that will aid your studies, all available from www.zidanepress.com.

Quote "stuff-special" and get 30% off normal price.
Buy Art-theory for Beginners and Philosophy for Beginners and get both for £10 (quote "stuff-speical2")

Philosophy for Beginners.

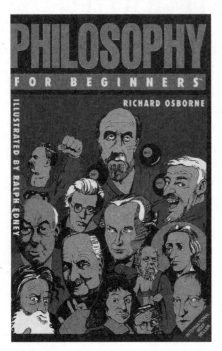

This introduction to all the main Philosophers in the Western tradition is the best basic guide to the big questions that all humanities students need to know, from Plato to Post-modernism. "This book serves as an excellent resource to familiarize yourself with the great thinkers.It's easy to read and laid out well, providing a student to the subject, easy reference.The basics are so well explained that you will have no trouble in selecting further reading material to deepen your knowledge." geraldine mary-anne moodley. Amazon co.uk

An international best-seller translated into over thirty languages, just published in China by Chongqing University Press.

Art Theory For Beginners.

This book delivers what it promises: a complete survey of all the historical and cultural debates on art. From palaeolithic cave-painting to Tate Modern, this concise and entertaining introduction offers the beginner a survey of all the debates that stem from the idea of "art". Philosophers, artists, theorists and critics are all included.

Being a second year fine art student, I found this book contained everything I needed to know about the history of art. The information is written and presented accessibly and gave me a brief overview of art theory. Its a perfect book if like me you are studying art and need some basic knowledge of its background to give you a better understanding of terminologies. It's also a good starting point to draw upon specific terms you may need for particular essays. E.C. Taylor-Davies. (Amazon)

"An essential introduction for all arts students"
Professor Marty St.James, University of Hertfordshire.

"This is a wonderfully clear summary of all the currant debates in art theory"
Professor Marina Wallace. Artakt, Central St Martins, London.